How To Lose Your Shirt Starting A Mail Order Business

How To Lose Your Shirt Starting A Mail Order Business

(From The Author's Personal Experience)

Joseph Lanciotti

Writers Club Press
San Jose New York Lincoln Shanghai

How To Lose Your Shirt Starting A Mail Order Business
(From The Author's Personal Experience)

All Rights Reserved © 2002 by Joseph Lance

No part of this book may be reproduced or transmitted in any form or by any means, graphic, electronic, or mechanical, including photocopying, recording, taping, or by any information storage retrieval system, without the permission in writing from the publisher.

Writers Club Press
an imprint of iUniverse, Inc.

For information address:
iUniverse, Inc.
5220 S. 16th St., Suite 200
Lincoln, NE 68512
www.iuniverse.com

ISBN: 0-595-24387-8

Printed in the United States of America

Disclaimer

If you lose your shirt by following the concepts of this little book it will probably be due to your doing everything that it warns you against. The author hopes that in addition to sound advice, it also provided you with some enjoyment in reading about his misadventures starting his mail order business.

Just one of these tips will save you the price of this book many times over. If the contents discourage you from starting a mail order business perhaps then too this book will have served a valuable purpose. If you read carefully and follow the concepts proposed herein you will not loose your shirt.

If you insist on continuing to pursue your dream of entering a mail order business this guide will not steer you wrong. If you make a million I'll be as surprised as you will be. If you have fun and make a little money besides, I will join in your good fortune.

Legal and accounting advice should be sought from your professional advisors and is not the intent of this book. You can read for yourself that none of that professional advice is intended or contained herein. I would not have the gall to do a thing like that.

Contents

PREFACE	ix
THE BASICS	1
THE PRODUCT	15
THE PRESS RELEASE	39
FRUGAL ADVERTISING	51
MAILING LISTS	69
DROP SHIPPING	75
LAST, BUT NOT	81

PREFACE

This book will tell you exactly what the title says, *How To Lose Your Shirt Starting a Mail Order Business*.

You will find the simple, basic steps to start a mail order business without glowing promises of becoming a millionaire as many books on mail order tend to promise the novice. Starting a mail order business is perhaps one of the easiest businesses to start, and attracts thousands every year, but it is not easy.

Most of the information in this book comes from my own study and experiences in starting a home-based mail order business. I wanted to be my own boss for a change. No one to answer to, to second-guess, to impress, and ask for raises. No boss or associates to suffer as fools. I was free to fly as high or as low as I pleased. I would call all the shots, gain all the rewards and take all the blame. I did not realize how much blame there could be.

Both my experience and time to write these pages cost me a bit of money and you can accept the advice or reject it. Whether you start a mail order business or not, the information in this book will be valuable to you as a beginner because it is written by a beginner, for a beginner, and does not assume that you know too much about the subject or have a large bundle of money.

You are an average person with drive who wants to start a business and you've got few bucks to get you started. You must be cautious, and you have come to the right place to find a conservative spender. I will part very reluctantly with a buck always remembering how hard it was for me to make it in the first place.

If this sounds reasonable to you, great. I will be talking your language and we'll save some money and have some laughs together.

If you read this book and find that the mail order business is not for you, (and for most people it should not be), then the book will have saved you countless hours of time and certainly some money. If you continue with your plan to become a business person for whatever reason life has dictated to you, follow the concepts in these pages with the greatest caution that is indicated to preserve your funds. Thousands of people every year find themselves in this last category for a variety of reasons. They just have to get into mail order.

I don't want to scare you away from your dreams and be negative about all aspects of mail order. Certainly there are many rewards in the mail order, aside from the possibility of making a little money, that are wonderful to experience in life. The first time you go to your post office box and find a bunch of letters accompanied with checks requesting your mail order products will be a memorable day in your life. Earning money is good, but the other aspect enter into the picture too, the feeling of genuine accomplishment.

Articles appear every day indicating that the first time business person has a tremendous chance of failing. Few last several years beyond start up, but the beginners keep coming up to bat again and again trying to make it work for them.

As the business owner you will become the boss, the manager, the supervisor, the floor sweeper, mail room person, advertising department, and all the other titles and functions rolled into one. You can take a lunch as long as you want, but I'll bet your lunches will be shorter than ever. You'll feel too guilty to spend time eating.

Sounds depressing? Well, it's the truth. That's why you're reading this book in the first place. You want the facts not pie-in the sky promises of how to start a mail order business in a quick, easy and inexpensive way and make a million dollars. This is a very basic book that will cover the areas the beginner will be involved in and I will lead you slowly and gently through the forest. Have no fear, I will be leading you cautiously into starting a business of your own.

If you start out making a lot of money from the start, remember, a little success in mail order can be a very dangerous thing. If you let it go to your head you will feel infallible and begin to throw away good money after bad, to coin a phrase. A small success creating a big head will eventually be more costly than instant failure. So let's take it nice and easy and stick our toes into the waters to get a feel of things.

THE BASICS

WHAT AND WHY MAIL ORDER?

Every one knows what mail order is. It is the selling of products through the mail.

Orders are solicited is a few basic ways such as advertising in magazines, newspapers, radio and television; and by direct mail by sending catalogs and flyers directly to potential customers.

It is a business that includes giant corporations, thousands of catalog distributors like L.L. Bean, Land's End and a thousand others, and more thousands of little people, like you and me, who may be around for a short while and then fade away. Sometimes even the big guys fade away when things are not managed right.

Mail order operations are conducted in large office buildings around the world and many work in little offices in their hometowns. This book is for the little person considering working from the basement, kitchen, or small office as many mail order beginners do every year. The business is so easy to start that it lures many people daily. It is a little like quick sand, it sucks you in slowly and gets you in deeper and deeper and demands more and more time and money to stay alive.

A recent documentary film on television indicated that mail order had sales of over 70 billion dollars per year in the 1990's other estimates that about 80 billion for the first decade of the new millennium. That's big business, and lot of people want to get into it everyday. However when you start talking about money of that magnitude it really does not sink into the average human being's head that it means real dollars. Billions and even millions are in a category that is beyond the scope of this book. Hundreds and thousands of dollars is what we will be talking about as much as possible.

Mail order is a flexible business that could demand enormous warehouse space, or a small basement space for office and storage. It is a business that usually has six or seven prime activity months for advertising and sales for the beginner. Usually the summer months are slow and used to find new products and plan the strategy for the coming months. The holiday season is awaited with expectation that could mean business life or death and that is a big expectation. The beginner will quickly note that from September to December of the year is big spending time and arrange to get into the action.

Starting in mail order from scratch places everyone on an almost equal footing as far as chance is concerned. There is no guarantee that any marketing approach or product will succeed. Many variables enter the operation including pricing, advertising, product quality, timing and luck. Everything being equal, everyone has a fair shot making little money and having fun in the game. The new comer should be cautious as I've said and will repeat until your sick of it. He and she must be frugal and hungry to learn. Read everything about mail order, even those, *How To Make a Million*, books, learn where to find products to sell and study the magazines to find out what is being advertised by others in the business.

UNCLE SAM IS YOUR PARTNER.

Yes Uncle Sam is our partner because we send him a share of what we earn every year. He calls it income tax. But in an other way he is a very important partner in the mail order business. Mail delivery and costs will impact on every thing that you send to your customers. The mail cost of sending flyers, catalogs and other information to customers will require consideration in your budgeting. Hopefully we can pass on this cost to the customer but we must not assume the customer will buy at any price. If Uncle Sam does not give us a fair rate, we lose our shirts that much faster. The cost of mailing has jumped up another three cents for the one ounce letter as this is being written and if I quote a stamp price and mailing charge one day, the book will be soon out of date because the price of mail will have gone up again and is not likely to ever go down.

You should rent a Post Office Box and use your box number as your mail return address for all those orders that you expect will be rolling in. Again start out by renting the least expensive box when you start out. If the little box you rent can't hold the mail you receive, the postal guys and girls will place it in a box for you to pick up for a while until you can get a larger one. Even the big boxes will get overflow orders at times and this is good news. If you find the box is too small you can always rent a larger one when needed and to keep the postal people happy.

The coming and going of the mail and the contents of your post office box will be a daily concern of yours the minute you enter the business.

"Did you check the mail today honey?" you ask your long suffering spouse, friend or lover.

And you'll wait anxiously for the answer.

Very often what is in the mailbox will set the mood for your day. When your mail box is full of mail orders you will feel fine and when it is empty you'll feel the opposite emotion. Lousy. In any case good old Uncle Sam will be at your side with the deliveries that are your connection with the outside world. When you rent a Post Office Box they will give you two keys. The cost of a small box at this date is under fifty dollars but I won't count on that price for long.

UNITED PARCEL SERVICE UPS

In some cases, depending on your product's size and weight, it may be beneficial for you to check the services of the UPS for a competitive price. At times their rates and delivery time can beat the Postal Service. (Forgive me Uncle Sam, but your know it's true.) Call the local UPS for all the information that you can get without cost about schedules rates etc. etc. They are always glad to help you and give you free information that will be important to you. Don't be afraid to listen to what they have to say about their operations.

The UPS has many services that you should check out such as pick up and delivery of packages at your office or home, but this will not be a problem of yours for a while. Just learn where the UPS office is and drain them of all the free information you can get. Do the same with Uncle Sam. Learn what the different postal rates are and everything else that can be of use without cost to you. Sometimes a small change in your mailing package can save you many dollars. A few ounces here and there are important and a few ounces can be saved in various ways.

Depending on what you are mailing, your product, you will require the proper packing to protect the item and to keep the costs low. You should investigate the padded envelopes and the bubble wrapping that is available a various stationary stores and compare prices and quality. Buy a small amount and test the mailing process to see how these packages work. Check with UPS and the Postal Service for any advice they can give on packaging and shipping.

LET'S GET STARTED

The first thing you have to do is develop a business plan. I want to get this out of the way because every Harvard Business School graduate who reads this book will check how I covered this important requirement. Some basics of business plans are discussed in chapter seven just to cover my behind with the Harvard experts. These are only basics so that at least you will have some knowledge about what a plan is and won't look stupid when someone asks, as happened to me.

One day when I went to a free consultation meeting with a SCORE representative in my area. (SCORE stands for service corps of retired executives.) It is made up of volunteers who work with the Small Business Administration at times, or on their own as volunteers who provide information and guidance for new business people.

When I went into the SCORE meeting a couple of distinguished gentlemen with silver hair smiled at me knowingly and shook my hand. They looked very self confidant and looked at me like they did not need me at all. And they didn't, I needed them. After all they were giving free information about starting a business and had years of experience as retired businessmen. They looked a little smug and conveyed the fact that they had been through it all.

After the brief niceties they got down to business.

"Do you have a business plan?", one of the silver haired gentlemen smiled and his eyes searched me for something that I had never heard of before and he knew it.

"A business plan? What is a business plan?"

I had already started my mail order business and wanted to get some free advice from someone who had been in it. Neither of the two men had been in mail order and they didn't care, business is business and a business plan is what they wanted to see. I didn't have one and that was the end of the consultation.

And they were right. They were right for someone who had the idea of entering a very structured business needing to borrowing bank money and charting out a program of costs and profits and all the other requirements of a business plan. Details of business plan development will take time and you can get help from several sources but I am not writing for that audience of mail-order beginner. I am assuming that you will not get involved with banks and other lenders of money other than your in-laws or second cousins who will not likely ask for a business plan.

So let's take the basic steps to form our own company and buy the equipment and supplies that will be needed to get the show rolling a little. You won't feel like a businessperson until you have an "office" and a business name.

To register your company name you must visit your county offices to fill out the necessary forms establishing a business. They will check out the name you have chosen for your business to make sure that it has not been assigned previously. Of course there are always fees for this service but the charges will not break you. They are minimal and that is a pleasant surprise.

You will need a copy of your business establishment forms to open a business checking account with your bank. Unless your are properly registered as a business in your county you can not open a business checking account.

When you chose a name make it short and try to make it reflect the type of products that you plan to sell. Don't give yourself some overbearing and pompous name than is easily detected as phony. You will be advertising in the classified sections of magazines when you get started and they charge by the word. Some magazines may charge several dollars per word and that could ad up if you have a name like, The Little House On The Prairie Gift Shoppe. Get the point?

Remember you may have only one or two products to sell when you begin but may add to our line later on. Try to choose a business name that would sound comfortable with the products you will sell. My mail order business name was **Overview Ltd**. and I used it for a variety of products and services I later sold and provided under that title. Overview Ltd could be selling dog toys or Bermuda real estate, or even iceboxes to Alaskans. I wanted a general sounding name that could fit many endeavors.

Find a good, kind, bank that will open a small business account for you. Don't take out a loan. If you need money to get started see your father-in-law or aunt Suzy, or better still, don't start until you have the resources. Get the basic check book with your name imprinted on it and chose a logo that associates your company if you can. I like lighthouses so I chose a lighthouse as my logo. That way whenever I wrote a check, the lighthouse and the name Overview Ltd. made a connection.

If the bank has those books with three checks per page book get it, and get a bank that will not charge you a maintenance fee if your balance goes below five hundred dollars if you can. Like the post office, the banks keep adjusting their rates and one day's quote may not be applicable for more than a week or so.

    Okay. We've registered the name, got a checking account and put several hundred dollars in it, so let's go out and spend some money. Order one thousand business size envelopes, stationery with your company name on it, and an address that includes a Post Office Box number, not your home number. You get the box number from the post office for a fee. Buy the smallest box and use one of those new checks to pay for it, or better still, use your credit card and delay the payment almost a month and perhaps get a credit card reward too.

    Staples is a good place for these supplies and while you're there get a thousand return envelops for reply orders, a thousand labels for mailing out packages, some bubble wrap, wrapping paper, five hundred business cards, a rubber stamp with ink pad. The rubber stamps can be made to read your address, paid, amount due and any other message you want. Then find yourself a good scale that will measure accurately from ounces to several pounds so that you can weigh your mailings before you get to the post office and play 'let's guess' and have everybody in line swearing at you.

    Get yourself a computer if you don't have one. If you do you can make your own stationery and flyers when it's time for advertising. I am assuming that you have a desk lying around and a chair to go with it. That's your office furniture. Add a table for packing and wrapping and other chores and you're on your way.

    All your printing needs that you can't do on your computer should be done at the quick copy outlets. Make sure the printing is professional and doesn't mark you as a rank beginner. No typos, no smudges, no misspellings if you can avoid it. Take your time and read anything you write over and over and then let your buddy read it too. Put it aside and then give it another read the next day.

    The computer will save you many hours of drudgery in keeping records and maintain mailing lists too. I don't think anyone is in business today without using a computer.

BUSINESS STRUCTURE

To keep things simple and easy I would suggest that you operate as a sole proprietor business not a corporation unless there are plus reason for your personal situation that makes a corporate structure more practical. I am assuming here that you are beginning and not one who has been in business before, and many of the things I say may sound simplistic to the more experienced businessperson. I'll chance that and keep to my target audience, the beginner with limited money to venture.

The sole proprietor business is the easiest to form and keep records and operate. As a sole proprietor your income tax forms will not change much. You will be required to add a Schedule C to the 1040 indicating a business operation. Any gain or loss will be added or subtracted from your personal income tax return. The income tax aspects of sole proprietorship can be rewarding but your accountant will give you details on this, if you have one. In all probability in you're first year or two you will probably operate with a tax loss, which you will deduct from your other income if you have any. One of the main disadvantages of a sole proprietor operation is that you as the owner are liable for all company debts, but if you have a loss it comes off the top, and that will make you feel a little better during tax time.

I could easily copy information here from government manuals describing the corporation structure and partnerships and all that other stuff you find in the big fat books that tell you how to become a billionaire in mail order but I won't. I figure that you are intelligent enough to know when someone is padding his book to make himself look smart and expensive by adding a lot of material that is available in many other publications for free. Remember that word, FREE, despite what they say, some things are really free and I will try to give you a list of them as we go along.

A very beneficial publication for small business people is the US Printing Office Publication 334, "Tax Guide for Small Business" Write for a **free** copy or obtain it from you local IRS office if possible.

This publication contains information about your income tax obligations. It describes the various types of business structures and the tax implication for each. Rather than copy it in this book I chose to have the reader order his own copy, which would be current and not dated with this book.

The Small Business Administration has a number of other publications that will be very valuable also. Write to them at 1441 L Street, N.W., Washington, D.C., 20416. Ask for the booklet Selling By Mail Order. This used to cost a buck or two and was very concise and pertinent. It contains some of the basic information on mail order that many of the fancy books being published today do not include.

Taxpayer Identification Number

You will use your Social Security Number as your taxpayer identification number required by the government. This number, in addition to being included on you tax return forms, is also used to identify you when you collect sales taxes for your state. You will send for the necessary state tax forms from your state offices that handle this operation. This is another bookkeeping operation that will require you to submit records of your sales and the tax collected on a quarterly basis to the responsible office. The red tape can be considerable and painful.

I cannot include information covering the requirements of the fifty state on collecting mail order sales taxes because it would take ten volumes or more. You know your state capitol. Just find out where the taxation department is and tell them you are in business and would like to know about sales tax collection requirements. My experience has been with the New Jersey taxation people and when I looked at the requirements for keeping records and collecting and sending sales money to the state I was nearly ready to stop everything right there. How the hell is a little business person working by himself going to get work done if he or she has to fill out all those forms and keep all those records for the government? I could not find the time to do it. The way the law reads today for mail order tax collection it does not require you to collect sales taxes if you don't sell to people in your state. There was discussion recently that that was going to change, but it did not and hopefully will not. If it does, many small mail order guys will be out of business.

NOTE: I would strongly suggest that if at all possible when you start your business that you don't sell to people in your state to avoid this added work and cost to you. When you establish yourself a little more and are more comfortable with your operations you can consider selling within your own state and collecting taxes as require. But send for the required forms and the procedures just to educate yourself on the tax collection requirements for your state.

SHOW ME THE MONEY

One thing I learned quickly when I started to research material for this book and began to operate my own business is that everyone seems to be making money. It seems no one wants to admit losing his shirt. That indicated to me the information they gave was purposely incorrect. That's another way of saying they were lying.

Another thing I learned is that there are many books available written by experts who are patting themselves on the back and giving "free", complicated advice for starting in mail order with all sorts of exotic formulas. They will tell you how to tests a product in the market with special mailings and advertising that will cost you thousands of dollars if you had it. You can test the product in various magazines, at different times of year, parts of the country and establish a program that will cost a bundle and still would not tell you anything conclusive.

These authors think they are speaking to multimillionaires who have unlimited funds to try their formulas for success. If some one has found a secret way to make a barrel of money in mail order or any other way for that matter he is not going to write a book and tell everyone how to do it. He'll keep it to himself. Then too, there are many who will not write about how they lost their shirt in starting a mail order business. They would be too ashamed. Everyone likes to feel that he came out at even whether he did or not. I have little shame.

You can ask anyone to show you the money, but they will hesitate before they do.

If you say I can make millions in mail order with little investment and little work, I say show me the money. Show me the money you made in that un-American way of no work and big gain.

You may follow all the good ideas in the world and do all the right things at the right time and still find that Lady Luck has not knocked at your door. But, that is true in most things in life, you must try our best and say, I gave it my best try. You can't do better that that. If your best try does not work the first time, give another try and perhaps another.

Make sure that you don't spend all your resources on the first try unless you're absolutely sure that it's the right thing to do. And don't kid yourself as we all tend to do at times telling ourselves that it was the best shot when we know we were only half trying. You better know when you're lying to yourself or you're in deep trouble. You better get that resolved before thinking about going into business.

We will repeat over and over that mail order is a copycat business in many respects and that is true for most businesses in the world. Look how well the Japanese have done on this management principle. The large auto companies copy designs, and electronic companies are constantly using each other's ideas. Coke checks out Pepsi and vice versa. When you see a winning ad in a magazine, one that is repeated month after month, year after year, check it out thoroughly to see why it is working for that person. Learn from it. Read it closely. Check the color, the design, the tone, the product, and the price. Then, when you prepare your own ad, use the principles of the ad you studied. You don't copy the ad verbatim, only to use the winning qualities with your own ideas.

The best secret or advice I can give the beginner in mail order is to be cautious and use common sense. Easy advice but hard to follow as most good advice is. When you find a product that you think is good to sell in your business don't get emotional about it. You can be enthusiastic, but emotion must be under control. This goes also for the magazine you advertise in. Don't satisfy your ego by buying expensive ads in a national magazine that will not return your money. You won't be able to sustain the cost and if you tried, there goes your shirt.

Squeeze the buck and hold tight to the pennies too. There will be many ways to spend as you go along but you must pace yourself. Take it slow but don't fall asleep and do nothing.

OFFICE EQUIPMENT AND SUPPLIES

You can save a little bundle in this area if you watch your step and shop around the used furniture stores and discount markets. First look around your home and those items that you are preparing for that garage sale may just be the ones that can serve as furnishings for you basement office. An old table or two can be used as desks or packaging tables for mailing your products. Check out that old office chair, the table lamp, the file cabinets, pencils, pens, paper, and anything else that you see as possible office equipment and supplies. Shop garage sales and you will save money fast.

The first edition of this book indicated that I was using a word processor rather than a computer to save money. Computers were quite expensive at that time but have now been reduced in price to make them a necessity for your business. If you don't have one, buy one. If you don't know how to use one. Learn. Take a course or have your teenage niece or nephew break you in with the basics. Even if you don't go into business, don't go through life not being able to use a computer. Once you do learn, control yourself and use discipline, don't spend all your time sending e-mails to friends and family. Remember you are in business.

The computer will save you time and money in creating letters, flyers, ads, and other print products you will develop. It will also make your mailing list easy to handle and your bookkeeping tolerable. A computer for your purposes at this date should not cost more than $1,000. If you have one already you are ahead of the game.

You can estimate that we have spent over a couple thousand dollars already without finding a product to buy and resell, or buying our first magazine ad. Thus far the computer is the major expenditure. The next will be buying products and advertising. We will get to that shortly. So much for those books that say you start this business on a shoe string and make a million. If you believe that, I have a bridge over in Brooklyn I'd like to sell you. Oops, too late, it's sold already.

The very basic, very conservative and cautious approach to entering mail order may amuse the experts who have written classic books on the subject detailing how to become a millionaire. Some of these organizations will sell you secrets and slowly pick your pockets, as you get in deeper with their mail order programs. Thousands of us are interested in mail order so these experts have a ready audience of receptive and often naive business beginners. You know, one is born every minute. Some organizations will sell the beginner lessons and then sell them products and catalogs to sell. These operations are of questionable value and should be examined very closely and used with caution if at all.

At this point, and we are only ending the basics section, you have been guided into the world of mail order without a lot of baloney about making a million and starting on a shoe string. You can see that there are quite a few things that you have to consider before you start and you had to have a few hundred dollars at least just to reach this point.

If you had ideas that you could start a mail order business with a couple of hundred dollars and selling a lot of junk merchandised from third world countries, forget it, and **stop reading this book**. You've already saved yourself a pile of money and time and should be glad to get the mail order idea out of your head. The Small Business Administration has a publication that suggests the beginner in mail order have at least sixty thousand dollars. However, I know you can do it with much less as I did, or you could start with much more, which I did not. It is impossible to say **exactly** how much you will need until we know the products you intend to sell and the scope of your intentions. The point is that you can control the amount you invest in the business without going overboard. That is the idea to keep in mind. You approach each phase of the business cautiously and make your decisions after considerable examination and thought. If everything seems reasonable so far stick with me and let's get into the subject a little deeper in the following sections. I promise you that I will be telling you only the truth as far as I know and won't be exaggerating or discounting information just to get you sucked in.

On the other hand I don't want to frighten you away from your dream of starting this business because it is very doable and rewarding, not only financially, but because of the pride and fun you will have knowing that you are in control of the situation as much as possible and are not relying on others to run the ship. It's a great feeling and a great satisfaction to know that you can create something on your own and control its destiny. Many thousands have wanted to try running a business and very few have ever even tried. That alone is something of immense value for the ego and for a life experience.

THE PRODUCT

BUYING AND SELLING

The world revolves around the concept of buying and selling things to sustain economies, create governments, and putting food on the table. Just think about it. Everything depends on the process of buying and selling products that are manufactured, grown or created by humans or animals or nature. Then around this action we form various side professions such as shipping, advertising, packaging, transportation, law and medicine and all the other jobs of mankind. But without buying and selling there would be nothing.

Mail order is based on the same concept of having something to sell. What you sell is the primary step you must consider. Products are available at gift shows in large cities, export houses, trade shows, manufacturing outlets and some are self-made. You are looking for a good mail order product and there are thousands. Not all of them are good. In my business I've sold simulated alarm systems, odor free garlic, and luggage, called The Seat Bag, bird cages, tweezers and many other things. I'll tell you some stories about these items later on.

Besides attending trade shows and examining catalogs for products, I contacted people I read about in the news who had developed a new item and asked if I could help them sell it. Don't be bashful. A man out in the Midwest got a plug about his plastic orange peeler from Andy Rooney on a TV show. Andy peeled an orange in one continuous peel and was done in a jiffy. The man was written up in many stories and told everyone that he was doing very well since he got the plug from Andy Rooney on TV. I know he was selling a bundle of those orange peelers which looked to me like a very good mail order product. I just had to check if the price was right and if the man would sell me some of his peelers. I contacted him, bought one to examine for myself and offered to buy others if I liked it. The man was agreeable and his price permitted me to advertise and make a profit when I sold them.

What I did was advertise the product in a classified ad with the hope of getting orders and then I would place an order with the peeler gentleman for peelers to send to my customers. I didn't buy a large quantity, only one, I didn't buy a full page ad, only a classified ad costing under fifty dollars in a homemaking magazine. When the ad drew customers, I placed an order for more peelers. You see, you take one little step at a time. If I knew that Andy Rooney was going to interview me on TV I would have bought much more, but that was not possible. So don't be bashful about contacting people who may have a product you think you can work with. More often than not the other person is glad to hear from you.

What To Sell

Are you going to sell those harmonicas and jade hairbrush sets made in Hong Kong? The harmonica plays three notes and the jade fades in two weeks. Folding hangers to save room in the closet? How about plastic flowers that you never have to water? The world seems to be revolving about a billion plastic products that imitate the real thing. Some people have made a fast buck from these items because there are a million buyers in the world looking for something useful and inexpensive. Many people in mail order, as in other businesses, sell dreams and promises instead of the real thing. I prefer to sell a product that can genuinely help someone, has a fair price and not junk.

Don't sell intangibles first and then offer tangibles as a secondary offer. Don't offer a plastic knife that doesn't cut and then try to switch your customer to an expensive steel blade that does. You should remember that to sustain your business, you will have to establish repeat sales and sell to customers for a long time on a continuing basis.

If you plan to push cheap products and go for the one time sale, you will not be around for long and will probably end up losing you're money faster than you make it

A Good Mail order Product

Once you begin thinking about mail order, you should know what product that you will be selling. Perhaps I should have covered this information in the first chapter, but it is so obvious that I felt that you would already have an idea of a product that you want to sell. If you do, fine, if you don't, not so fine, but read about the basics I suggest and then see if it makes any sense.

The basic qualifications generally for a good mail order product are as follows:

    1. Have a good markup potential. (That is, buy something that you can resell for a large profit. I could give you a percentage markup to shoot for, but there are variables to consider too. Sometimes a smaller markup is acceptable if the volume you sell is large. Only you can decide this and at times it will only come to you after you've tried selling the item for a while.

    2. The product should be easy to package, and mail or ship. Consider the postal fees and UPS fees that will be added to the cost. Don't, for Pete's sake, try selling anvils or any items of this heavy weight without considering the negatives.

    3. Your product should have wide application, a large potential buyer crowd. Find something that will appeal to many people. Something for both sexes, something for young and old, something for fat and skinny.

    4. The product should be available to you on a continuing basis. Your supplier should be as reliable as you can find because you may returning to him for reorders. If you have a product that you make or control yourself so much the better. I'll explain a little more about this factor in the following pages.

New products are fine but define "new". Few things are completely new today. They are variations of the old. Is the product durable and well made, easy to use and attractive? These are good points to consider. Sometimes, if a product wears out under normal use, it is a good feature, which will promise follow-up sales. But the product should not fall apart because it is poorly made. These products will only give you aggravation when your customers return them for refunds and you establish yourself as a junk seller.

NOTE: You can't fool all the people all the time. You may cheat a few at the beginning but it will catch up with you, as it should. Sell good quality products, sell at a fair but profitable price, guarantee what you sell and back it. This is very good policy in any business, but sometimes even the big shots forget this simple principle. Your product may not have all the features to make it perfect for mail order, but it should have some. The more good features the better, although you may be able to succeed in selling a product which qualifies only for some of the above attributes.

ESTABLISH A PRODUCT LINE

If at all possible try to find several related products of good quality instead of trying to make a go by selling only one item. Usually, you will find an opportunity to sell additional products once you find some customers who are satisfied with their first purchase. Try to develop a line of related products, house wares, security, auto care, pet care, etc. Try to find products that are not available in the local retail stores (this is a difficult thing to do). You'll find that manufacturers sell to the large chain stores to get their products introduced to the masses, as is every capitalist dream. If you find a product that looks good to you, first check that your local supermarket or department store is not selling the same thing at prices that you can't compete with.

If you have the wrong product, you'll find that everything else with your operation will go wrong and be expensive. And painful. Don't fall blindly in love with your product and overlook its weak points as we are apt to do with lovers. Have your friends check it out and give you their honest opinion. Don't be sensitive to criticism. Make the product prove itself to you in every way.

NOTE: For heavens sake, don't start advertising a product that is already available in your supermarket at half the price. You can't compete with super stores and add advertising costs to boot.

Your enthusiasm for a product will be contagious to your buyers as you prepare exciting ads describing it. At least I hope it will. If you are not enthusiastic no one else will be either. Being enthusiastic is one thing, in love, is another.

Later on when you have made your first sale you will have to follow up on the customer with other offers. You should be mailing flyers for other products in your line. Try to judge what the customers is interested in from what he has bought previously, but note that you can never know exactly what a customer will buy so don't assume he would not buy a product that you have in stock. Offer him everything you have to sell and keep your fingers crossed.

Some mail order companies have been founded on a products that are especially made for the mail order operation. Selling herbs and teas by mail have been very successful when accompanied by clever advertising and the product stands up to its reputation. Some mail order operations stock products the owners made personally such a decoy ducks, fishing lures, booklets and cooking recipes to name only a very few. If you have this type of product that you create yourself and it may appeal to large group, you may have an ideal product which is under your control.

Once you have found a product that you are satisfied with that will meet the criteria for good mail order potential, you'll have to decide what you want to price it and where to advertise. Remember that the price can be changed as you go along, and you don't have to stick with the first price you chose. If you find a higher or lower price is better for sales, price accordingly.

Some people test several prices to determine the response rate for each. But it is absolutely necessary to set a price that will return your investment with a good profit. Do the simple arithmetic. Determine the cost of your product, advertising and shipping and set a price that will give you a good profit after your expenses including your time.

If the quality of the product is good, and the product unique, it may warrant a higher mark-up than usual because there will not be another product to compare with it. Markups of over 1,000 percent are possible; so don't be afraid to make that kind of profit if your product is especially unique and warrants it. In most cases, however, you'll have competition from similar products and that will drag the price down.

BEWARE OF COPYCATS

When you find a good product and it is setting the world on fire with sales, you can bet your bottom dollar, or just your bottom, that you will have a lot of competition soon enough from copycats who will try to reproduce your item at a cheaper price. They will be studying your ads in the magazines just as you are studying theirs. If they see that you are running bigger and bigger ads every month they will get the idea that you are pulling in the bucks. It would be a good idea be calm and disperse your ads among several magazines at that time and not get too large a profile as to attract too many copycats until you have worked the market for yourself.

The longer you are in control of the product and the longer you are supplying the market by yourself, the better it will be for your bottom line. You will find out soon enough when your market has tired of your product. Your mail suddenly begins to fall off. You may get a false ending period first and then another upsurge so don't take the first decline as the end of the action. Be patient and stick with it for a while, try another ad approach, try another magazine, but don't go overboard. You'll find that when it's really over pretty clearly, and then its over. Get on to the next priority.

NOTE: Stick with the winners cut the losers free. This is the same advice they give those who invest in the stock market. This is easy advice to give, and sound, but for some reason people have a problem in taking it. Don't keep trying to push a product when it has given you every indication that the market for it has dried up for any number of reasons. If a product continues to bring in business, why drop it?

Case History

At one of those big trade shows in New York at the Jacob Javitts Center I came across a product that was being offered that looked like it was a quality item made in the USA. It was called the Miracle Point Tweezers and was used to remove very small splinters or hairs with its very sharp point. The tweezers were small, inexpensive, easy to ship, and had a large market potential. (It could be used by both men and women of most all ages.) The dealer offered to sell the tweezers in small quantity so that I could test the market without buying a truck load and risking disaster. It looked very good to me.

The supplier also had some nice looking sales sheets or flyers that could easily be printed with my company name and save costs for direct mailing. I asked if I could use his flyers with my name on them and he agreed.

The next thing I plan with a new product is a press release that I send to publications announcing the new product and hoping that I'd get some free exposure. I have never failed in getting some announcement of a new product in a magazine or newspaper. The trick is picking the publication that is best suited for the product you are selling. You don't sell knitting items to muscle building magazines. Make sure that when you send out a press release on your product that you send it to a magazine that would be interested in it.

So you see the initial expense is low. I go to the free trade show, (they usually let you in if you have a legitimate business and have a business card.) I buy a few inexpensive tweezers (or other products) with the idea that I will place a large order if they sell well, I use the suppliers flyers with a little inexpensive quick copy printing to include the information I want to add, and I prepare a press release.

I send the press releases to newspapers and magazines and newspapers all over the country but not more than thirty or so. One goes to the Associated Press writer who is looking for products for his column, another goes to the wood working magazines that would be interested in tweezers to remove splinters, and I may even send a release to a first aid magazine that could use a new product story. When these press releases are printed the readers will send for further information or even send money for the product directly.

If they ask for information, you send them a copy of your flyer that you reprinted from the supplier's original and now include your company name and the product information that you added to it.

The orders start coming in from all over the United States and sometimes from around the world. What fun. My mailbox is alive with the sound of money from the tweezers sales. I felt I had a good product. No, I did not have orders for millions or thousands, but I did have orders for hundreds and that was a good enough start for me. I had only invested a small amount of money and it was proving profitable.

My supplier had sold me the tweezers for $1.25 each and promised that I would get additional supplies as needed for the same money. I started selling the tweezers for $3.95 and when demand increases I raised the price to $5.95 for the new customers. I thought that this was a fair price for the tweezers because it had some unique features and was well made in the USA. Also I had not seen it available in local stores including drug stores which were sure to carry this item if it were good.

The orders continued to come in so I placed a larger order with the supplier and found that as I placed larger orders he charged more for the product. It should have been the other way around—the more you buy the less you pay. No way Jose'. I knew I was at his mercy and that he could cut me off at any time unless I found another supplier which I tried to do without success.

If you run out of a product and the orders keep coming in there is only one thing you can do. You must do. You tell the customer that you are out of product and return the money. You disappoint the customer and yourself as well, but that is the only thing to honestly do.

I chose to continue supplying my customers and making a smaller profit as the supplier charged more. In the meantime I continued trying to find a new supplier and even a manufacturer who sells to the supplier. No luck. I checked libraries for manufacturer directories and even asked my supplier boldly who his source was. He laughed at me. I felt trapped.

One day I was in a local chain drugstore with my dear wife and what does she say to me?

"Sweetheart," she says, in that voice of panic and fear knowing what she is about to tell me will upset me, and I will blame her for my misery. It has happened before so she knows the odds are against her.

"What is it!", I asked fearing the tone in her voice that I had heard many times before when disaster was pending.

"Look", she said pointing to a large bin of tweezers at the front of the store. "Miracle Point Tweezers."

My heart dropped.

An enormous tub of tweezers for less than half the price I could buy them was being offered by the chain drug store. Was it a loss leader? What did these little tweezers mean to this large chain? They had thousands of products to sell and they bought their products by the truck load. They did not go to the trade shows and dicker with the venders for a free sample, or buy a dozen, they had the resources to buy everything they wanted.

I had to find another audience for my tweezers supply before the chain stores had reached all the customer potential in the country. I asked myself, who in particular besides the family would need these tweezers? The answer was wood workers, hunters, and fishermen. Why not advertise those magazines? That's what I did. I took out classified ads in these magazines and introduced the tweezers to an audience that may not have been near the drug chain store.

I sold all the tweezers in my inventory as fast as I could because I knew that its time was limited as my mail order product. You notice that you have to be on your toes and use your head in mail order. You don't have the luxury of filling bins with products and have people come to you to buy them. You have to reach out to your buyers, track them down and show them that you have something they want and need. Of course if you have big money you can open your own chain store.

THE SUPPLIER AS AN ENEMY

If you missed it, let me point it out to you again. You must find a supplier who will work with you and is true to his word. This is possible for a short time, but over the long period it is impossible. Suppliers go out of business too, they have to reduce their prices to large buyers, their operating costs rise as they do for others and they pass on those costs. They can't make a living selling small quantities to mail order beginners.

You must be nimble and quick like Jack who jumped over the candlestick. When you are small you have the advantage of changing the course of your business without too much cost. You don't have big budgets and a board of directors to consult and worry about. You move at your own fast speed and get in and out of a product as quickly as necessary.

Having a substitute supplier is fine if you can locate one. At times several suppliers may be able to get you the product you need. That is a plus for you. You can bargain the price between them. Remember you can never be absolutely sure about your supplier coming through with what you need. Buying in larger quantities is often possible to protect yourself from loss of product availability, but it would be wise to try to have a return agreement with the supplier. Some will grant return credit others will not. You have to work this out by yourself but don't end up with too much inventory you can't move.

Trade Shows For Profit and Fun

Trade shows are held every month throughout the United States. If you live near a large city, you will have access to these shows which are attended by vendors and suppliers who are trying to sell products. These shows are good for evaluating products, finding product leads, and getting information in general. You will meet people from all over the country who are in business to sell. They will usually be glad to talk to you, especially if you show an interest buying their wares.

When you attend these shows for toys, gifts, books school supplies, whatever, try to keep an open mind and not gravitate to those products that interest only you. Consider the taste of young people, and women and children or, men, if you are a woman. Think senior citizen and what they will buy. Listen to the supplier and talk as little is possible. You learn more when you listen than when you talk.

Ask about shipping methods, bulk buying costs, advertising, and track record of the product if it has one. Learn all you can about the product and the vender that you can.

Once you have attended a show, you will be placed on a mailing list, which will inform you every time they have another show. Also you will be on a mailing list that will send you information on trade shows throughout the world.

You've joined a fraternity and sorority that constantly are in touch with you to remind you of their affairs and wanting you to join with them. I've always found that these trade shows to be very enjoyable and meeting various people from all over the world is fun. The shows also give you a chance to travel a little and they are a business expense for tax purposes. So. Please keep your expense records straight and have a good time too.

Some Don'ts and A Do

Don't sell products to your neighbors you would not use yourself. Don't make false claims as to the products benefits. Don't worship your product and fall in love with it. Don't sell food, clothing, and drug products. **Do** have a money back guarantee policy.

Shipping and Handling

When you've found your product you should examine it closely to determine what the handling, packaging and shipping requirement will be. This is very important for your bottom line. Once you decide on the packaging, try it out and see if it is feasible. Is the packaging operation easy to accomplish, is the box or wrapping inexpensive, is the weight of the package reasonable?

Try to visualize your entire operation from beginning to end. What tools and material will you need for shipping? How about bubble wrap for protection? How about a tape applier and extra wrapping tape? Make a list and head out for your local Staples store and buy cautiously. Don't overstock, buy sales, look for discounts and return policy. We're talking serious penny pinching here.

Once you find your product or products and you are getting responses to your ads, and the orders are coming in, you should have a small supply of the product to fulfill orders. But, don't overstock and take a chance that the supplier will work with you for a while. If something happens suddenly that you are cut off form a product, don't panic. If you have orders that you can't fulfill you just have to send the money back and explain what happened. It all probability this won't happen but if it does it's no big deal. You are not cheating anyone.

You will need a fairly large area to prepare for shipping of product orders when they arrive. Try to visualize that your mail box had twenty to fifty orders for a variety of your products. You've opened the envelopes and arranged the checks according to the product ordered. You made sure the amounts were correct and that they included shipping and handling charges. Now you arrange the various products on our shipping table and organize the shipping containers for each product. You have boxes, wrapping paper, bubble wrap, shipping labels, and tape machine ready to go. You've got to create an organized way to proceed or you will end up making mistakes in shipping and taking too much time.

I would suggest filling out your shipping label first and give it a code for the product that goes with it. Then I would place all the same orders together. You will then know how many of each product you will be handling, and can arrange your packing material accordingly. Pack all of one product first and go to the next until you are done. If this sounds simplistic, it may be, but it is important too. After packing you will be ready to go to the post office for mailing. Visualize tomorrow bringing in another fifty orders, followed by twenty orders, and so on. You can see how the work will pile up and get confused if you don't have a system and ship promptly. The bad news here is good news, really. You can also visualize the mail box being empty every day and you don't have a shipping problem.

NOTE: **Remember when you are shipping a product you must ship within thirty days or inform your customer of the delay.** It's the law. If possible send your product out the day or following day that the order is received. Also when you ship your product include a flyer or other literature offering the customers another product or products that they can buy. This little advertisement travels for free with your delivery package and is a good way to keep your customer thinking about buying more.

BEST BUSINESS MONTHS

Some products will sell better at different times of the year. If your product is seasonal, don't advertise it during the off months. Remember you have to give your magazine display ads some lead time before they are printed. (Three months lead time is about right.) If you plan to advertise in the December issue they will want your ad approximately three months ahead of the print date. Classified ads may be scheduled in a shorter time frame. Display means the ad has some artwork or design in it and usually a border from an inch or two or full page.

Once you get started and are advertising in several magazines it would be a good idea to make yourself a calendar indicating when your various ads are appearing, in what magazine and the date.

April	Sunset Magazine	classified	product	cost
May	Home and Garden	display	product	cost
June	Popular Science	classified	product	cost
Sept.	Yankee	classified	product	cost
Nov.	Farmer World	display	product	cost

(Add any information to your chart that you feel is of value.)

Remember there is a lot of competition out there, billions of dollars worth they say, and your little product line is just entering the water to test itself. I would strongly suggest that you get yourself down to the nearest library or Barnes & Noble and look through all the magazines you can. Read the ads for mail order advertising. Study those ads and memorize them, especially those that are similar to your product.

Check the back issues and see how the ads have changed and what months are not used for ads and what moths are. Check the holiday season ads especially, that is the time that the win or lose results will be made.

FINDING A NICHE

Low product cost alone will not guarantee you a successful business. You've got to reach the right market first. You've got to find yourself a niche that you have carved out for yourself. Many books and reports will tell you that selling books that you write and produce yourself are the best products to sell by mail order. There are many writers and printers who are in this niche already but there is always room for an original and talented person in this area.

I'm not talking about large novels, but rather small, How To, booklets to help people in a variety of situations. How to buy a car, how to fix a roof, how to clean windows, how to make money in the stock market. No, forget that last one, there are too many books about that subject already.

In this type of operation you become the manufacturer, the supplier and the seller all rolled up in one. There are companies that will sell you their own How To books for you to market on your own. I have not examined the value of this type of operation but would suggest that that you examine it completely before getting involved. Examine the product. Is it something that you would buy? Even so, buy in small quantities and don't lose your shirt.

The best way to sell How To books is to develop your own if you have the ability to write, or work out a deal with a writer who can do it for you. However this can be complicated and we are trying to keep away from complications.

If you can develop a series of How To booklets of real interest to the general public or even to select groups you may have a potential mail order opportunity which you can control completely.

If you have only one product to sell, it will be difficult for you to remain in business for long. I know, I've said that before, too. Although a unique and profitable product could work out alone, the potential for added profits with additional product sales to offer is so great that it would be foolish not to have related products to offer your customers along with your lead items.

There are thousand of stories about successful mail order people who started with an idea and a dream and made it work. Here is another to add to the collection. The names are fictitious to protect the rich and famous.

John and Jane Doe loved square dancing and were very interested in attending dances and competitions around the country. They got to know the professionals and the people who just enjoyed square dancing for the fun of it. You wouldn't believe how many thousands of people there are who love to square dance, attend square dance competitions or just watch as entertainment.

John and Jane found out that they had a large American audience that enjoyed the same dancing and would be willing to buy square dancing records and tapes. They established a part time mail order business, making tapes and records and selling them all over the country. Then, they added other products to their line, including books, costumes and a newsletter, all on square dancing. This was their niche and they excelled in it.

I met Joan Roberts when I answered an ad she had placed in the local shopper looking for someone to help her in selling her ski products. She sold creams, oils, to protect against the sun and wind, she sold head bands, and a variety of items of interest to the skier. Joan was in her forties, tall, attractive, an avid skier who was on the slope every chance she could get. She belonged to various ski clubs and loved to travel to ski resorts all over the world. I liked the sound of her voice over the phone and her enthusiasm and decided to meet her to hear her story and determine how I could fit into the picture.

Joan told me that she had started her part time mail order business seven years ago. Right off this impressed me a lot. Because there was few start up businesses around for seven years, and I knew that she must be doing something right. What Joan was doing that was right was selling skin lotions and protective ointments to men and women, a large audience. She had developed several sales sheets that she had inexpensively printed which listed her products and prices.

As Joan attended her ski jaunts, she would distribute her literature to those she met or tacked them on the bulletin boards or left them in the shopping areas or wherever they would be picked up. Over the years, she had established a large mailing list of buyers who were also her friends at the ski scenes.

Joan was not out to make a million dollars or to work too hard because she had a good job as a teacher and wanted something associated with her love for skiing. When she retired, if the business was still going well, she would continue it full time. In the meantime she had found the way to make a second income, and also to reduce the cost of her ski trips because she could write them off partially as business travel and expenses.

I get a big kick, and a little pain in the rear, when I read the books on how to make millions in mail order. They talk about testing the market with intricate mailing tests that would cost you thousands of dollars to try. They suggest taking display ads in magazines that would cost you another bundle. Who are they writing for? Surely not the beginner with a limited bank account. Do they know what it costs to advertise in national magazines, or even in small regional magazines? Another bundle. Another shirt loser unless you are careful and frugal.

You can see the people I've met in the business are the little people like I am, who work hard, did their homework and entered the business cautiously. Whatever success we've gained was not by learning "secrets" of mail order or investing big money to test, advertise and sell products. We don't have that kind of money. We learn, work hard, and plan over a long period of time to establish a viable business and we spend cautiously and frugally. I love those words.

A unique aspect of the mail order business is that you can start it on a part time basis without anyone pushing you to speed it up. You can set your own pace and feel your way along the dark roads cautiously and not get hurt by shooting from the hip and making snap judgments.

Besides giving you a lot of so called secrets, a lot of books on mail order presume that you have a bundle of dough to spend and lose. Even the better books suggest an operation that will cost the average beginner several thousands of dollars that he may not have. A book I saw in the local Small Business office estimated the beginner should have seventy thousand dollars available to start a business in mail order.

Yeah sure. Seventy thousand dollars! If you follow the outline they suggest, with all the bells and whistles, you'll need ten times that and more.

What I'm anticipating in this book is that you don't have that type of money and that you are starting small and hungry, but you must have somewhat more than just a shoe string.

If you are looking for a quick way to make a ton of money this is not the way to go.

THE TAIWAN CONNECTION

I met my good friend, Tom Wong, at one of those Rotary meetings I attended as a guest to hear a speaker talk about import and exporting. As luck would have it I was seated next to Tom whose English was and still is unique and at times mysterious. One must listen closely to catch on to what Tom is trying to say in English. Most people who listen to him come away without learning very much because they did not understand most of what he was talking about.

Perhaps that is why I was seated next to Tom, not luck, but no one wanted to spend the meeting listening and nodding pretending that he understood what was being said. As a guest, they did not think it would bother me for one meeting. And it didn't. It turned out that it was one of the most rewarding meetings that I ever attended and I met a man who, if you listened closely was very interesting and savvy. I asked Tom what business he was in after we had gone through the singing and hand holding required of Rotary meetings and were beginning to have lunch.

"Import and export," Tom said.

My ears perked up. I knew he would not ask me what my business was, so I told him right off and did not waste time.

"I'm starting a mail order business," I told him. "Do you know anything about mail order?"

"No, I rike sell my products that way. I have products from Taiwan but don't know how get advertising." Tom said, in more or less in these words.

Tom has a perpetual smile on his face and always breaks out into an easy laughter whether he gets the joke or not. When you tell him something funny or tragic, he smiles and laughs It is his way of being polite. He has been in this country over thirty years but still feels like a stranger and apologetic for his lack of language skills. His skills as a human being are excellent.

I asked him if he had a business plan. He was still smiling but I don't know if it was because of my question or just part of his usual happiness.

The smile was because of my question. He understood what a business plan was. He had a PhD in business from Cornell. I learned this when I got to know him better and he added to his personal story which he loved to tell.

"My family in business over one hundred years," he said, "we don't need business plan we have family plan."

It turned out that his grandfather had started many businesses in Taiwan and importing was the latest of many ventures that the Wong family found interest and profit in operating. Tom was the oldest son in the family of five girls and one younger brother who was ten years younger than Tom. Since Tom had come to America and the younger brother remained in Taiwan, the day to day control of the family business was in the younger brother's hands but that did not mean that the respect for the elder son was forgotten. As number one son he carried a lot of cultural clout which extended into the business world too.

He talked about the family which was involved in various business ventures and you can imagine how large the family was when he referred to number nine uncle and number seven uncle, remembering the members of the family by number rather than name.

I had lived in China for over a year after the war and understood some of this culture and also spoke a little Mandarin, which I studied with a private tutor during my year there. Mandarin is the official language and educated Chinese and Taiwanese usually understand it along with their own dialect. But being Taiwanese and very proud of his birthplace, Tom preferred speaking Taiwanese rather than Mandarin.

I tried some of my best Mandarin Chinese on him and he looked at me without smiling and said, "What you say?"

I had asked him if he spoke Chinese, "Nee quey dshaw tsoonga wah, ma?"

I was hoping that he would compliment me on my accent as many Chinese restaurant waiters had done, even if they lied.

He had not understood a word, or pretended not to understand as he often did when I attempted to speak Chinese to him. Then his smile returned to ease my embarrassment. It was with careful consideration that I attempted Mandarin with Tom again, and before I did I would warn him what I was about to do so that he prepared his ears for my brand of Mandarin.

We talked a little about importing and exporting and how similar some of the problems were with mail order. He picked warily at his chicken croquettes which swam in a yellow sauce that was unfamiliar to him. He had mistaken chicken croquettes for just plain chicken. He did not know what croquettes were but was saving face by not complaining. He left most of the meal on his plate.

I offered to write a press release for one of his products and arrange to place a classified ad in a magazine. He was advertising in the local daily paper with display ads for his product called the Seat Bag and it was costing him his shirt. Reluctantly he accepted my offer but indicated that he was off to Taiwan in a couple of days and would not be back for several weeks. I thought this was his way of stalling and saving face by refusing to take my offer, but it turned out that in two weeks or so we got together.

His smiling face greeted me when I entered his office and we talked about his trip and his family which he loved to discuss. He and his brother had taken over their family business in Taiwan which manufactured various products which were sold to dealers who had contacts with Kmart, and other large stores, and also with horse trainers throughout the world. Tom was trying to sell the Seat Bag which his brother was manufacturing in Taiwan and selling very successfully in Europe.

I gave Tom most of the advice that appears in this book about building a line of products for a target audience and I also bought some of his products to sell through my own mail order efforts. The Seat Bag was one of them. The first press release I wrote for the Seat Bag was used in the New York Times, and Tom was very impressed. I continued consulting with him for many years while still operating my own business, but we were able to be of mutual benefit to each other in many ways.

Tom got a big kick out of making sales to people from all over the United States and the other parts of the world. When we first started together he bought a large map of the States and every time we made a sale in a particular state he would stick a colored pin in the state on the map. He used different color pins to indicate amount of sales. It was not long before the map was alive with colored pins. Once just for the fun of it I removed a large red pin from Colorado on the map to see whether Tom would miss it. I never believed he would miss just one of so many pins.

But he did.

"Where is Corrorado pin," he asked me in annoyance one morning and I could not help laughing at being caught in my deception.

He was annoyed and said, "you joke me." But his usual smile returned and he joined in my laughter as he added another pin to Colorado where it belonged.

I told Tom to use 800 toll free phone service for his customers and it worked very well with increased calls coming in and recorded on the answering machine when we were not in. Calls would come in from all over the country and included many of the accents that would give Tom trouble in understanding. When this happened he would call me.

"Herro, Uncle Joe?, theese ees Tom." He would announce to my answering machine, and of course I would know immediately it was Tom.

Most times I would pick up the phone and he would not have to leave one of his long messages which ended with the plea, "Prease call me."

He called me Uncle Joe as a matter of respect since I was several years older than he, and looked even older because he was a very handsome, slim and young looking man with jet black hair, and I am rather portly, shorter than he and mostly bald with a little gray.

He informed everyone that he dyed his own hair without any loss of face. He felt it a necessary thing to do.

When I was at home and answered the phone in person most times the conversation would go like this.

"Herro, Uncle Joe, theese ees Tom. May I speak to you?"

"Yes Tom, what's up?"

"What you mean what's up? nothing up. I have question."

I explained what "what's up" meant and then asked, "What is it?

And then he would tell me about the calls he received for orders or inquiries and that he had difficulty in understanding them and would I come into the office and help him.

"Of course", I said, and would be into the office within a short time. I loved the mail order business, the talking with nice people from all over the country and being able to sell them something they would enjoy. I loved to get letters thanking us for the product and for our service. I loved to make money and have Tom make money almost as much, and at times more, because that smile on his face was payment enough for the help I gave him. I believed too that he would gain greater proficiency in the language and be able to carry on this phase of the business in a short time by himself. He did not, and we were together for a long time.

After almost ten years of our association I would still get that phone call which I expected almost every day, "Herro Uncle Joe, theese ees Tom. May I ask you a question?"

I would know that there was a mail order question to be solved.

And off I would go to resolve the question he had.

In retrospect, at times, I begrudged that time spent with Tom and his All Seasons Products because I had business of my own to attend. The hours of phone calls, designing brochures and flyers, placing ads in national magazines, making sales, mailing products, arguing and having fantastic Chinese lunches, and hearing stories about Taiwan and the Wong family, ate into my time, but all in all, I know it was really the best of times. As I was trying to build my small mail order business, searching for products, placing ads etc. I was breaking Tom into the mail order procedure too. He already had access to a variety of products and really was in a better position to start mail order operation than I was. His big drawback however, besides knowing very little about mail order, was proficiency in the English language.

THE PRESS RELEASE

General

Press release, or editorials as they are called by many in the mail order business, are relatively simple, quick and inexpensive to prepare. Thousands of press releases are prepared every day to announce events and news of much, little and no consequence. A press leases may announce the election of a president, a raise in your property tax and the election of the local dog catcher. Thousands of releases are sent every day announcing a new product on the market and the magazines are interested in these stories if they have at least some news.

All these releases have the same purpose in mind, to get free space from publications. A well written release with at least a bit of news interest is always a possible winner for magazine or newspaper space. The trick is to write it well, briefly and pack it with as much news as possible without lying.

Press Style

Write your press release in the newspaper style with the main point up in the lead, the first paragraph. Use clear language and include interesting facts for the readers of the publication.

Note that the main part of the story is covered in the first paragraph or lead and in each succeeding sentence the story unfolds. The name of your product is in the first paragraph but your address is at the end. The editor will decide whether to use your address or not. They usually do, but it is his decision and his favor to give or not.

Usually when they use the story they will mention your company name and also your address and the price. The reader then can contact you with an offer to buy or for additional information. In any case you have made a sale or possible future sale by sending the release. I would estimate that I've had about a 50 percent success rate with my releases and I'm not a magician. They do work.

Notice too that the name of your product is used many times in the body of the story to establish it with the reader. Boldfacing the name is also a good idea.

No press release should be more than one page unless you genuinely have news that is fresh and important to the editor. If the news is of marginal value, keep the release brief. Use your own stationery for our releases and include your telephone number in case the editor wants to ask more questions. If you have additional information, like a data sheet of your product, you can send this to the editor for his information in case he wants more, but do not attach it to the release. The release stands by itself. Some mail order people have sent product samples along with the releases but I never have. A sample cost you mailing money and product money and may offend the receiver. Unless you have a very good reason for sending a sample I would not.

Is It Real Turtle Soup or Only The Mock?

Is the release you are sending really of any news value at all or only an imitation of news? If it is mainly imitation, you must examine it closely and extract whatever news you can from the piece. Sometimes just adding a word or two that tailors your release to the publication you are reaching transforms its importance. If you have a cutting tool, it could be a fisherman's cutting tool, or a hunter's cutting tool, or a hobbyist cutting tool. In this way you appeal to specific groups and it is now news.

When you identify the reader of the magazine in your release you are making the news for him interesting. A product may be presented at many levels of interest if it has multiple applications. If it does, then present it in a variety of ways.

Give your release a very good editing before you send mail it. Write it like a pro, check your spelling and grammar. Check again for the value of your release to the publication that you are sending to. Have you read the magazine to see the type of products and stories they use? Does your release and product fit in with the rest? Send it out.

If your release has real news value with a new product or service that has wide appeal, you won't have to worry about getting it printed. The publications will be competing with each other for your story.

So, if you think that you really have a winning story to tell in your release, take some time to prepare it and then send it out to as many publications as you can. Make sure that you give the facts and don't exaggerate the value of your products in the release. This is not the time for fiction writing, but don't be too timid either.

Let's Write One

Let's assume you have a product you want to bring to the market. You've found it in a gift show, at a manufacturer's show, in a magazine, any where. I don't care where you found it. That's your business and don't tell anyone else. Let's say it's a pot holder with heat protective fibers that protect your hands when you use it to lift hot object like cooking pots. (I just made this product up.) Don't get too excited about it. A pot holder is a pot holder. So what?

Well let's explore this pot holder for a minute. Special fibers? Sounds interesting, if true.

Let's call the product The Hot Mitt. It protects you from burns while cooking and baking or barbecuing. That involves activities that many men and women are familiar with and the product should have wide interest.

Let's explain what the product is made of and what it can do for the user. It is made of a combination of metallic and textile fibers tested to withstand high temperature of over 600 degrees for fifteen minutes before allowing the heat to come through.

Now let's write the release based on these "facts".

IMMEDIATE RELEASE

       Contact Abby Smith 555-556-5678

NEW PRODUCT ON THE MARKET

HOT MIT is a new product on the market for cooks, bakers and housewives who cook indoors and out. It protects your hands from high temperatures because of a new textile and metallic weave that is incorporated in the glove.

Developed by John Kirk, a renowned chemist, the **HOT MIT** was patented last month and has been tested by laboratories throughout the country. **HOT MIT** is made of fiberglass and zinc alloys that are woven into a process that reduces heat conduction and can be cleaned with ordinary soap and water.

HOT MIT is available by writing to Overview Ltd., 555 Ely St. Wood Rite N.J. 070778. They are $9.95 a pair plus $2.50 for shipping. Checks or money order.

NOTE: The last paragraph contains the name and address of your company and the price of the product. A reader can order the product or send for additional information based on this release.

If warranted, we could add another short paragraph to describe use of the product. In this case it is not necessary and in any case the release would be only one page long.

Now Target Your Audience

Who would be interested in the HOT MIT release? Persons interested in cooking, or if not, perhaps interested in making a gift of the product. Go to your library and ask for the media list from the reference librarian. The directories will list many magazines and other publications that may use your press release. Look through the copies of magazines in the library and read the ads and editorials to determine if they use your type of product. If you send the release to a newspaper make sure that you send it to the food editor or the living styles editor. (In smaller papers one person may handle several departments in the paper.) The media lists in your library will list the various editors and the departments they service, so this is no big deal to find out.

If your product warrants it, take some good black and white photos of it to send with your release. Photos are always good to introduce the product further. You don't have to send photos to everyone you send a release to because this would cost a bundle. Pick your best possible publications and send the photos and release to them. There will be many publications that you could send to but try to set your priorities for the ones most likely to use it.

Have someone proofread and edit your press release thoroughly. There is nothing like a bunch of typos or a misspellings to mark you as an amateur.

Most of your releases will not see publication and that is to be expected without being too concerned. Enough will be used to provide you with leads for future sales or make direct sales immediately. If the release is used in a newspaper or in a wire association, which is usually syndicated, you can expect to see the printed version in a week to several weeks depending on the editor's space demands and interest. Magazine usage of the release will take a little longer and your chances of getting picked up by a magazine is not as good as for newspapers, but magazines will use the release if it is to their liking. You have to realize that the magazines comes out usually once a month and the newspapers are printed daily so the space to be filled by papers is much greater. Newspapers are usually hungry for *good stories* even if they come by way of press releases.

If a magazine, uses your release and the results are good with many responses from buyers for product or more information you may decide to place a small ad in that publication. Magazines are geared to provide classified space for mail order sales while the newspapers usually are not. Magazines tend to be read by several persons before they are discarded and are kept around the house for reading longer than newspapers. You have to consider that to have your ad get maximum exposure.

A very good approach to magazine advertising is first to send for a Media Kit from the magazine's advertising department. The Media Kit will include free copies of the publication, information on the advertising cost, publication dates, readership population and many more important facts for you to decide on when placing an ad or even sending a press release. Remember it costs you nothing. The advertising department is glad to get new business and will be after you to help you with your ads. All magazines have Media Kits so don't think it is a big deal.

Many magazines have a section called New Products or a similar title which features information on new products of interest to their readers. This is the area you will aim your press release at. Some magazines have an editor supervise this section and refer to the New Products Editor. Address your release to this editor if he is listed in the magazine masthead. The masthead is the front of the magazine that lists all the editors, and other information concerning the publication. Read these sections in the various magazines and determine what they require. Then tailor your releases to correspond. If your product is photogenic, that is, has some photographic interest and is not just a wire hanger or something like that, take photos and send copies. A photo and a story in this section of a magazine can be of great value. Black and white photos usually work out better for these purposes than color, but I've used both and usually had both available to send with my releases. Your product photos should be sharp and professional looking, and sized at two by four or four by four inches.

NOTE: Call the 800 number printed in the magazine and ask for the advertising department. Give your company name and tell them you're in mail order and are planning an ad for their magazine. Give the young lady your company name and address and she will send you a Media Kit. Don't forget it, do it.

I introduced you to Tom Wong after I met him at the Rotary Club meeting. I told Tom I would buy his Seat Bag, write a press release, and send it to the New York Times. He smiled and I knew that he did not believe a word of it. Both he and I were very happy to see the Times use the press release, and then many other papers all over the country used stories about the Seat Bag that we included in other releases.

The Seat Bag was a good mail order product. It was small, approximately 18-inch square when open, but folded to about two and a half inches by 18 inches square and fit into a shipping box that looked like a small pizza. We had these boxes especially made for shipping it. The Seat Bag was a nylon, olive green, carrying bag on a steel frame that folded and formed a seat when open and could support over 300 pounds. You could carry it by shoulder strap which was supplied, or by the steel frame that folded up when the bag was packed and formed a carrying handle. It weighed less than four pounds, and could be used by men and women, young and old. It sold for $39.95, including shipping and handling. Press releases about the Seat Bag were sent to many magazines and newspapers and were printed very often.

Sometimes a wire service like the Associated Press will use your release or part of it and when they do it is usually picked up by many other papers that subscribe to the wire service. You are lucky when this happens and you get the added publicity. When letters came in from Seattle asking for information about the Seat Bag we knew one of the Seattle papers had picked up the AP story that used our press release. We would then follow up with other releases to publications in that area, and also advertise in magazines that cover that part of the country.

Remember that press releases cost little to develop and send out and the possible gains are many. Be sure you write the releases in a professional manner and choose the best publications to send them to. There are too many publications to send releases to, so you better discriminate and choose the ones that you think will return the best results. Try to decide which would be interested mostly in your product. If you're sending to wire services likes the AP don't worry about spending a few cents on any extra stamps. The possible rewards warrant most releases being sent to them because they may be used by many other newspapers that subscribe to the wire service.

Study the Media Kits for the publication style and needs. If your products look like they belong in that readership category send out the press release.

Now read the following closely and understand what I am saying. One product may be marketed under various names because it may have several applications. Tom Wong's old Multi Purpose Seat Bag that I wrote a press release about and sent to the New York Times was exactly that type of product. It could be used by a varied audience. Over a period of years the Seat Bag assumed a variety of names such as these: The Pilot's Seat Bag, The Artist's Seat Bag, The Golfer's Seat Bag, The Hunter's Seat Bag, The Bird Watchers Seat Bag, and so on. We sold this product to bird watchers for years and then changed the name to target other interest groups as noted and advertised in the magazines that reached these groups, but birders and artists found the seat bag to be a good product for their applications and we sold it to them very successfully.

THE BIRD WATCHERS SEAT BAG

I like birds but did not know much about them. Tom Wong told me that in Taiwan many people called any bird, "a bird", and that was it. There were not the many hundreds of designations that we use in this country to identify the many birds in our country. Blue Jays, Robins, Tangiers, Hawks, etc. etc., in Taiwan, according to Tom, were just, "bird", and what's more they were considered delicacies and good for the many recipes on the island.

"That's barbaric," I said.

Tom would give me a sad smile that was a little embarrassed, but then recover himself.

"Different culture," he would say defensively.

"Barbaric," I repeated.

I had suggested that we expand the name of the Seat Bag to, The Bird Watchers Seat Bag, and try to reach the large bird watching audience in the country. He thought it was worth a try, but never showed any real enthusiasm for the idea. We placed several small display ads that cost about $250 a month on average, for a couple of inches of display space. Things began to happen.

We began getting many orders for the Birdwatcher's Seat Bag which we advertised in *Bird Watchers Digest, and then in, Bird World, Birder,* and other birding magazines. We had reached a potential audience and began to scramble for other products to sell in this birding line. *The Bird Watchers Digest* magazine really reached the audience we wanted and the Thompson family that published it was very helpful.

BIRDING TRADE SHOWS

The Bird Watchers' Seat Bag became a well known item to readers of the birding magazines and to people who sponsor birding shows around the country. We were invited to attend these shows to sell our products. The booth rentals were reasonable and within our budget and we decided that we would attend our first show which was in New Hampshire.

Attending these trade shows are a lot of work but also a lot of fun, and I considered this part of mail order very interesting and enjoyable. It gives you an opportunity to see another part of the country and meet new people. It gives you a chance to talk to others in the business and meet potential customers. We met mail order companies who specialized in birding and were able to get our products, including the Seat Bag, into their catalogs. This turned out to be a good deal for us since it gave us wider exposure in catalogs that we could not afford to print for ourselves at that time.

Some people at the show were interested in selling their products and we contracted to add a few of their products to our inventory. The atmosphere at the shows as far as we were concerned was very friendly and everyone was cooperative and helpful.

We had rented a van that would carry our product samples which at time also included spotting scopes as well as the Seat Bag, ponchos, and walking canes. You see, we were building a group of birding products so that we could reach a wider audience. You must expand your product list and not rely on one or two products to continue your business as I mentioned before, I know, I know.

Tom and I, and our wives, Sue and Vivian, went on this trip to Manchester and between us we manned our booth from 8 in the morning to 9 at night. Besides selling products at these shows you have the opportunity to hand out literature and meet other distributors who may have interesting products too. We exchanged ideas and information and enjoyed ourselves to boot. If you can't participate in the show as a vender, try to attend as a visitor and make contacts that way which can be rewarding too.

I would strongly recommend that the new mail order person check out local trade shows and gatherings that can be attended at reasonable cost. There are so many special interest groups that meet periodically and if your product can be of interest to them you should make yourself known. Set up your products, literature and any other equipment that will help you to make contacts. This can include photographs, slide presentations and audio displays. Just watch your budget and check out the costs for value. Unless the show location is in a large city the prices, in my experience, were reasonable. This is a decision you will have to make for yourself.

If you have a special interest in the groups that you are trying to sell to you will have the added benefit of enjoying yourself immensely.

The four of us attended a meeting of birders in Cape May, New Jersey, a very popular birding location, after we attended the trade show in New Hampshire. This Cape May meeting was more for instructional purposes for new birders, but we went along to make contacts and add on to our mailing list. At these meetings they will usually list all the attendees and their addresses and this is valuable information for you to know. As I said, if you develop an interest in the sport or activity that your customers are participating in you will gain that much more in business and in life.

In our product line, including our all star Seat Bag, which had many applications, we had the opportunity to attend dog shows, horse shows, art shows, poetry and musical events. There was always an opportunity to show off the Seat Bag and other products and to enjoy the activities. Attendance for these shows does not cost you an arm and a leg. They are very worth the attendance in every way.

One birding event in Virginia was especially enjoyable and rewarding business wise for the three day attendance required. Renting a tent to display and demonstrate our products, we were located in a beautiful part of the Virginia coast overlooking Chesapeake Bay. Good views, good food, good friends and good business are the memories of that event. Need I say more?

THE ARTIST SEAT BAG

Tom Wong is a talented water color artist and loved art in general. He was also an accomplished pianist. When I suggested we try selling the Seat Bag to the Artist community as The Artist Seat Bag he was very agreeable. We could not think how we could sell it as the pianist seat bag, or we would have tried.

The most successful audience it was marketed to was the artist. The Artist's Seat Bag sold very well over a period of years. Some of the other applications did better than others, but the artist community was the most active. The important thing here is to understand that you can market a product to a variety of groups if it has a function and value in each area. This holds true for many products that have the possibility of interest in many applications. We advertised the Artist Seat Bag in The Artist Magazines for years with success and developed a loyal following. We would not try to sell The Birdwatchers' Seat Bag by advertising in Artist magazine. We had to change its name and describe it in a different application to fit the artist. If we told the birders that they could fit binoculars in the seat bag, we had to tell the artist that he could do the same with his brushes. It only makes sense.

This will simplify your efforts considerably as far a press releases go. You change a few words, like Artist for Birder, and a few words in the lead of the release, and you are in business. Your product becomes associated with the target group you are aiming for, and has more impact.

The American Artist saw many of our display ads printed over the years and so did other artist related magazines. We built up a following of satisfied customers who sent us testimonials on our various products and recommended our products to their friends. Many artist groups touring Europe and other artist oriented regions like South America and Mexico used the Artist Seat Bag and sent us testimonials for our product. Many of our subsequent sales emanated from word of mouth testimonials. When you find a good product you will know it, because your customers will know it and help make it a success.

FRUGAL ADVERTISING

GENERAL

Advertising is a word that may conjure up visions of sleek, jet-set men and women catching a cab on Madison Avenue, New York or in giant cities throughout the world. We've seen Hollywood depict the brilliant, aggressive and attractive advertising people working on multimillion dollar deals and making tons of money selling everything that Americans want. Well, this is not the advertising world for the startup mail order businessperson like you who is going to squeeze the budget so tightly that your fingers will ache with the release each of the dollar.

Advertising will be the biggest budget buster that you will encounter when you begin business. If you don't watch out it will eat you alive. I hope that frightened you because I have every intention of doing just that. For some reason I don't understand, all the mail order books I've read have shied away from the cost of advertising. Unless they cover it at the level of corporate giants that spend millions. There are thousands of magazines in publication and only a fraction on the stands that you can see. Many are specialized publications that are mailed only to subscribers and not sold over the counter. Magazines cover every topic and activity that you can imagine. As soon as a new activity appears, a new magazine will emerge to service that sport, hobby or whatever. If your product serves a particular group, you will be advertising in the magazine that group buys.

The bigger the circulation of a magazine the more it will cost you to advertise in its pages. Those that have circulations in the millions will have some very big hitters vying to place ads in its pages regardless of the cost. This will not be you when you begin. Later, when you are an expert, it may well be.

For you, as a beginner with a very conservative approach, your world of advertising will be relegated to the shoppers section at the rear of the magazine which serves most mail order advertiser. No large TV ads, no radio shows, no full page ads in national magazine. Sorry, but then, don't feel neglected. Although you are not on the cover, the rear section of the magazines is where the mail order action is and it is not cheap to buy space there either. A two inch display ad in this area can cost you close to a thousand dollars or more in some of the national publications. The classified pages will run you from under a dollar to several dollars per word depending on the magazine. Nevertheless, this is the only place to start any advertising when you are beginning. Become very familiar with this part of the magazines. You will be living there.

There is a reference books in your free public library that will list all the magazines in the country and the research librarian will get it for you. You will see that some magazines list their prices at a very low and tempting rate and others are rated at an exorbitant price. Now this may sound like common sense, and that is exactly what it is, not rocket science, but plain common sense that is sometimes harder to understand by many people. Ask yourself why is this publication's rate so inexpensive? Look for your answer under its circulation claim. Low circulation, lower ad rate. Now, is that a good buy and the place to spend your money?

Ask yourself what area does the magazine circulate and does it reach the people who will be interested in your product? When you find the answer to these questions that suits you, check it against another magazine in the same price range and circulation. Which gives you the better deal? Use the toll free number of the magazine and call the advertising department and double check their circulation claim. Ask about previous mail order advertisers who were satisfied, ask about free rate for first time advertiser, no deal?. Ask for reduced rate, ask for reduced rates if you advertise three months, no not consecutive months, you want October, November and January or February of the following year.

You must ask for discounts, freebies, and other perks that may or may not be given to you. If they are, you are ahead. Sometimes a publication will reduce an ad cost for variety of reasons they will not explain. Most reduce costs if you advertise for three consecutive months but not for non consecutive three month periods. But you can ask for a concession and see what happens. Many times the rules are bent a little to accommodate the customer, but the customer must ask for them.

CLASSIFIED ADS

Everyone has read a classified ad in the local newspaper and is familiar with those long columns of text that sell every thing from baby carriages to Cadillac's. This type of advertising is essentially the same in magazines. These ads only contain words to describe the message and no artwork or photos. If you use artwork and or photos you have a display ad and that will cost you more money because you will be requiring more space.

In newspapers they charge by the line to place ads in the classified sections and in the magazines they charge by the word. From pennies a word to dollars a word. Let's say you are in a publication that charges ten dollars per word for your ad. That's easy to figure out what it will cost you for ten words. $100 bucks! Just try explaining your product in ten words, and oh yes, your company name and address count as words too.

Try using twenty words and it will be easier of course but then you have parted with $200 for that one time shot in a magazine classified ad. That will get your ad in the publication for one issue. For a newspaper you are in the paper for one short day. People tend to read magazines for several days at least and pass them along to friends and family and sometimes even to the Salvation Army where they will be read even more. The idea is that you have a better chance of being read in the magazines than the news papers for mail order ads.

As a beginner, you will probably use a classified ad as your first venture into mail order advertising because it is inexpensive compared to display ads, and it is quicker and easier to place since you don't need an artist to lay it out or create it. Also, when you use a display ad, you usually have to give the magazine three months lead time for printing, so you've got to plan ahead and run the ads according to the magazine's printing timetable. Once you are educated in using the classified section you will graduate into the display ads very quickly and we will get into the details of that area shortly. It is a little tricky, but not magic by any means.

Classified ads using words alone may be used to make a direct sale. The first printing brings dollars into your mail box with orders for your product. More frequently, the ad will result in a query for more information about your product. If readers buy your product directly from the information that you presented in the first ad, that is good news. Perhaps that will be all that you will need to continue selling, but I doubt it. Usually you will have readers sending requests for additional information concerning the ad you placed. Then you must follow up with more information describing the product, its use and condition of sale.

You must always include an **"Unconditional Guarantee"** for thirty days at least.

NOTE; An important point about classified ads is that even if you don't make a sale on the first offer, you've added a name to your mailing list which you can contact on future offerings. You will not always be able to determine exactly what a customer will buy. When you make a direct mail offer include all the products you have to sell and let the customer decide. You will be surprised at times what a customer will buy after you think you have him in a particular category.

Some products such as books and How To booklets—which I have sold with some success-and some failures- may be sold directly. Readers will not often ask more details about your offer to sell a book

For example:

> *How To Lose Your Shirt In Mail Order.* This book tells you how *NOT* to in 125 pages. $9.95 + $2.95 s/h 30 day money back Guaranteed. Checks or C/C's Overview Ltd., Box 211, Dept. 56, Loxi, N.J. 08084

If you placed this type of ad in one of those **"Find Success,"** Magazines, and there are many, that carry ads for beginning business people you could possibly sell directly from the information presented. I have. But the point I'm making is that a simple ad in the classified section could return dollars directly without further effort on your part other than the mailing and shipping of the product.

Some products will require that you sell them in two steps if you can't describe the product and the sales arrangement in one ad. First, you advertise the product, then you get an inquiry for more details which you send in the form of a sales sheet or letter. When someone responds to this ad with an order, you follow through with delivery of the products. It would be wise to stuff your product mailing package with literature about some of your other products for your customer to purchase. It goes free.

Many books on starting a mail order business will talk about selling you secrets of the trade. Secrets of Mail Order Success. What secrets? Can you imagine writing a book for thousands of people to tell them a secret or two. If you have a secret you keep it to yourself. That's why it's called a secret in the first place. Once you told thousands about it and they in turn tell thousands of others, the secret is no secret anymore. Right? Of course it's right.

One of the so called big secrets of mail order that many try to sell you as their own is ,"To make money and become successful in mail order you must find a product or service that has a universal demand and which gives complete satisfaction. These products are used daily, and bought repeatedly, by the same customers." Some secret. It is almost like telling you that if you make a car that runs on tap water you will make a fortune.

KNOW YOUR NEIGHBORS

Studying the classified pages of all the magazines you can get your hands on will provide you with a very good education concerning what is going on in the mail order business and who is in it with you. Not all of the ads will be professionally prepared, but if they are repeated every month over a long period you can assume that they are making money selling the product advertised. You can learn what is wrong and what is right about the ads and try to use the points that are beneficial to you.

Especially check out those ads that are promoting the products that are similar to yours. How is the ad presented, how large is it, how many times is it repeated during the year? Learn from them.

In starting, you will find that you will have your hands full in placing several ads at a time in various magazines. You really must develop a schedule of publication dates that will chart the name of the publication, the date of printing, and the cost. As the publication is printed you can track how the ad pulled for you and keep a record of the response that you get from each ad that you place. Don't try to keep this information in your head because it will be impossible and confusing.

Hopefully the publications you have chosen to advertise in will result in sales of your product. Make it your business to know how the magazines you advertise in work, who the readers are, and what the circulation is. If you have acquired a media kit as recommended earlier you have that information that the magazine sent you. They are anxious to get this information to you, and they want you to succeed so that you will continue to spend money with them. A failed business does not help anyone.

If you have placed several ads that will appear during the same period you may want to key the ads so that when the orders come in you will know which magazine was pulling the business. You'll see ads in the classified sections that will include something like DeptK in their address so that when someone responds they use that designation. This tells the advertiser the order came from a particular publication and a particular mailing. DeptH may be the key word for another publication or mailing. If you have several ads running it is important to know which are successful and which are not. The keying of your ad will help you to find out. You can use any code or symbol for your address in your ad. Just remember to keep it simple and you will pay for the word according to the magazine's rate.

Most times the customer will indicate to you where he saw your ad. It is good policy to note which magazines are giving you the action and keep a record of it. The code system further pinpoints the publication responsible for your business.

Magazines are good publications for mail order because they are written for selective audiences who have certain tastes and interests in common and provide an identifiable market for the mail order advertiser. This is true, however, the response you get from an ad is determined by many factors, including how an ad is written, what our product is, when the ad appeared and the price of your product, to name as few. Generally, if your ad has been designed to sell merchandise, a return of two to three times your advertising investment could be considered a good return. You are a lucky person if you get it.

You will soon be building a library of publications to study for your own advertising campaigns. In the meantime you can also go to your library to study the magazines on their shelves. Read all the classified ads and study the wording. Notice the action words used, "act now", "don't delay", "opportunity", "special offer" etc. etc. Try writing an ad for your product and check it closely. Keep the ad short but clear. Have someone else read the ad for an opinion. Be a severe critic and ask your friends to be candid about the ad's content. Sometimes we write an ad and assume it has clarity that it does not. Be careful and edit your copy several times until you are satisfied, **then edit it again**. This is tedious but absolutely necessary.

Your purpose in using classified ads is to gain attention and hope the reader will send for more information. If you make a direct sale from the ad take it as luck. Notice how often the other advertisers repeat an ad. If they use the same ad every month it must be making money or someone may be losing his shirt without knowing it. Check back issues of the magazine for the same advertiser. Notice some advertise every month and others disappear after one issue. This tells you another story. A sad one. People do not last long in the mail order business, especially if they keep making mistakes.

DON'T FALL IN LOVE WITH YOUR PRODUCT

One of the first products that I fell in love with in my own business was a plastic spout which I found at one of the annual gift shows in New York. This particular show was held in the Jacob Javitts Convention center which hosts many merchandise shows throughout the year. It is an enormous place and several shows run consecutively. These shows bring together many people who are in mail order and other businesses looking for products to sell. It was there that I found this little plastic spout that was a good product, but I should not have fallen in love with it. I'll tell you why.

When you fall in love you make decisions with your heart and not your head. It's the same as falling in love with a person. When you find a product that you think will be good for your business look at it with a cold practical eye and make sure that you are not giving it more affection than it is worth. If you do you will tend to over advertise to sell it and spend more money than necessary. Have some of your friends look at the product and evaluate it, and when they do, don't turn a deaf ear when they give you the bad points. LISTEN!

The Little Spout and Display Ads

I tell you this now with a little embarrassment but I want to save you the same pain. I fell in love with this little silly plastic spout just as sure as I fell in love with my fifth grade teacher. I'll never forget the experience, the pleasure and the pain. Clean lines, innocent looking, smooth texture, small, light and photogenic. Both the teacher and the product. The little spout had all the attributes of a mail order product that we demand. It was small, lightweight, and easy to mail, low cost, reusable and also replaceable. It was a milky white color and had a cute little red cap to protect its top. What the spout did was very easy to understand. You twisted it into a carton of milk or juice and it held tightly without leaking when you poured out the contents. This permitted you to pour out the contents without tearing open the top of the container. It was neat, clean sanitary, and attractive. I was sure the every home in American was waiting to buy these spouts from me.

I bought a quantity of the product and ran ads in Family Circle, Sunset, and other big hitter magazines which cost me big bucks for my classified budget. I paid too much to advertise a low cost item that sold for $4.95 for a package of three. I had a good mark up after buying the spouts for thirty cents each, but I was paying over $800 for a two inch display ad. I had to sell a ton to break even. I did not. I sold many but not a ton.

The ads were attractive but I don't think I told enough about the product to have people buy it on first reading. I should have tested the ad with my friends to see what they thought, but I didn't. Mistake number one. In one ad I forgot to mention that the spout came with a protective cap. That was another error that would possibly have been caught by another reader. I should have advertised in cheaper magazines to conserve my advertising dollars, I should have marked the product up a dollar more, I should, I would have, I could have, but I didn't. I promised never to fall in love again with a product I barely knew.

Really you can't count something as a loss until you've added all its possibilities for profit. Although I lost money on the *Family Circle* Ad, the experience was necessary to enter the game, I keep telling myself. Now, if I you learn from this experience without losing money, so much the better for you. You can go on to make your own mistakes and may they all be small.

Good Months, and Bad

There are rules, and there are rules that are broken. Mail order people generally feel that June, July, August and December are the worse selling months of the year for mail order selling. Supposedly people are out in the sun or planning holiday celebrations in these months and gifts have been already bought or not being considered. According to the statistics May and September are better for selling, followed by October, November, January, February, March and April.

Usually you will find that the cost of ads increase during the better selling months, but not always. There are exceptions for every rule and mail order can be full of exceptions to many so called rules, but you have to draw a line somewhere. So we make general rules and hope they cover the majority of the situations. If you have a seasonal product and it sells well in the summer, hey, good luck to you. Be careful that you have checked the product out for the use intended, and give yourself the lead time necessary to get your ad out to the readers at the right time for them to buy.

Generally speaking, for the little gal and guy starting mail order operation six months of the year will be better than the other six. Rather than spin your wheels without having a line of products to sell I would use these slow months to sharpen the product line and planning for the hopefully busy months ahead. Attend shows to check products. During your first year or so you will be spending more time learning than doing. At least I hope you will or perhaps do both together, learn and sell.

SALES GUESSTIMATING

There are all sorts of formulas for forecasting possible sales and many of these formulas cost a lot of money to try. For example many large and rich companies may test various advertising around the country to determine the market climate for a product.

They will advertise in several magazines at a time at various prices to see which pulls the most. After trying all methods they come up with an "idea" what the product will do, but they never know exactly.

As a beginner you will not have the resources or time to do this type of market research to test your product. If I've said this before, good, I've said it again and it is information worth repeating. The beginner must do some very cold calculations on how much is spent on the products, the marketing and the shipping costs, and his other overhead expenses before he sets a selling price. This is not that complicated. It just requires common sense for the most part, but a lot of beginners just do not do the very basic arithmetic.

If you buy a product for one dollar and you advertise to sell it spending $1000 dollars, you have to sell 1,000 products at $2 just to get your advertising and purchasing dollar back. (Product cost $1 X advertising per each product you are selling $1,000 = $2,000 if you bought 1,000 units of the product at one dollar each.)

Now you have $2,000 invested in the product and the advertising, not counting incidental office costs, and your time. If you sold 1,000 units at $2 dollars each, you recover your money. At $4 dollars each you recover your money and make $2000. Simple? Yes, but only in theory because it is very difficult to sell 1,000 units of any product. Don't take it for granted that if your ads reach two million people that two percent will read it and buy your product or that a half of one percent will buy it. In most cases, you just will never know unless you test the product over and over to build some kind of track record for it, and you're not about to spend that type of money when you're just starting out.

The percentage of sales from a very large mailing is very small as is the percentage of sales in a million circulation publication. That is why it is very important to zero in on your target audience as much as possible. That is why also that you should not have large inventories until you have proven the worth of the product.

After your ad appears you should get 50 percent of your responses within the first 30 to 40 days. Summer ads, if you place them, may be a little slower in drawing responses because people are not likely to read the publication as fast as in the winter months, but most of the responses will be in by 45 days. It is not unusual to get a response to an ad a year or several years after a magazine has been published. Some people keep their copies for a long time and believe that the ads are always viable. Even if you go out of business you can be sure that some time after that event a customer will send you an order.

One day we got a call from a lady in Utah (800 numbers encourage calls from all over) who said she had an old copy of Artist Magazine and it carried an ad about the Artists' Seat Bag. The ad was seven years old.

"Is the price still $19.95?", the lady asked.

"Sorry, no", we said. "The price has gone up".

She hung up.

NEGOTIATE AND LEARN

Everything is negotiable to some extent and advertising rates are too. Talk to the advertising department of the magazine you intend to do business with and ask all the questions you can concerning rates, placement of ads, sizes and any special considerations that they have for the small advertiser. Learn all you can about the magazine and always ask if the price could be made smaller in some way.

If you have a display ad that requires some artwork indicate that you will be preparing this ad yourself and you should get a 15 percent discount on the advertising rate. (You can get a free lance graphics person to layout your ad for you if you can't do it yourself.) If you are preparing a display ad make sure your artwork is line art or that the photos are halftone so the magazine can print it. Any free lance artist will know how to do this for you. Ask the magazine advertising department what their requirements are, so you can inform your artist.

Note too that if you run an ad for several months you will get another discount from most magazines. Ask them about it if they don't have that information in their media kit. Ask for a particular position in the magazine if it appeals to you and try to bargain for it. Ask for the top of the page if you want it, otherwise they will give you what they want and it may not be the best location. You should ask for everything you prefer and although you don't get it you know you tried.

Testing, Testing

There are many ways to test your ads and the possible success of selling your product. Some cost more money than others to try. Guess which ones I will cover here? You're right if you said the cheap ones. Testing costs money and those who test are not going to tell you which test were good or bad for them, or if they did it would not do you much good because circumstances change. You must find out for yourself.

I would seriously study the magazines you propose to advertise in and look at the ads for products similar to yours. How large is the ad, how often is it run, (every month for the year or only once), is the price the same as your product? This information will help you.

Some magazines suggest testing two ads in different runs of their publication. One run is mailed to one section of the country and another to a different section. You then test the response from two reading segments of the country. This is called a split run. The ads must be keyed so that you know where the responses are coming from, but that is no big deal as we discussed earlier. You can use two different prices in the ads if you are interested in testing the price reception, or you can test the ad itself by making each a different format. This sounds plausible to me, but also very expensive.

Varied responses may be the result of many variables so you won't want to change the ads too much if one ad pulls more than the other you want to be sure you know why. If one ad pulls more than the other, the winning puller must have had the qualities that the reader wanted. Was it low price or the ad design? Try to come up with an answer and then repeat the winning approach.

This is simple testing that can be made more complicated and detailed but will also cost as lot of money. When you are more established, you can explore detailed testing and probably develop methods of your own. No one will know more about your business that you do, and as time goes on, you'll learn to refine all the knowledge so you'll work faster, cheaper, and more efficiently.

I had an experience with a product that I advertised, and the manufacturer of the product also advertised in the same magazine but in different months. His ad was larger than mine, and he told me that he broke even. I don't know whether this was true or not, but I'll tell you that my ad cost me over one thousand dollars and I got less that one hundred dollars in sales. I'm not going to make a lot of false claims about the value of both ads, but mine was done by a professional artist and it was sharp and clear while the other ad was unprofessional.

Both ads offered the same product, with the same price, and with the same claims. Why not, it was the same product. I made several mistakes with this ad and this product. First I was competing with the manufacturer who made the product and could sell it real cheaper than I. Secondly, I did not have a large enough mark up to cover costs even if sold. Thirdly I ran ads in the same magazine as the manufacturer, who, in the long run, could undersell me and control the buying price. Those were a lot of errors that cost mucho dinero.

If the manufacturer of the product is also going into the mail order business to complete with you he always wins price wise. He can always beat you there, but there are other ways you can have the advantage, however, I would be cautious using them against the guy who controls the product. In a situation like this I would go find another product unless you can reach some sort of agreement with the manufacturer as to where your advertising will be submitted.

Also to protect yourself from increasing prices, try to find another supplier of the product. Competition is a great leveler.

I won't tell you that this is a secret or not, but it is a good idea and ideas are worth checking out. When you find another mail order company selling the same product you are, find out where the competition is buying his product so you can compare prices. You can do this is by buying the product from the competition. Sometimes the manufacturer is printed on the box. If not, contact the person you bought from and discuss the product and try to get information that way. Sometimes it works and at others it doesn't. It is worth a try.

At times you will find that you may be paying more for your product than your competition because he is bigger and buying in quantity. There is not much you can do in that situation other than perhaps advertise in a different publication if you can. If the product is returning a good profit you may as well stick with it regardless of the price.

What Is Success?

There are so many variables that will decide your success or failure, and if you are not cautious your money can soon disappear. Everyone knows the success story of the person who started with $50 and became a millionaire. Yeah, yeah. But no one writes about the thousands of people who quietly loose their shirts and silently pass into the sunset. This holds true for many business, but there is something about mail order that particularly seems to grasp the imagination. Perhaps it is the idea of independence that nags at us, and too. Perhaps it is the ease with which one can enter the business. But make no mistake about it, the road to success lies pave with the bones of many who have preceded us with the same hopes and dreams.

A Chance To Win

There is a chance to win at the game, but you must be cautious and plan your moves slowly and with a lot of common sense. Squeeze your bucks, cut your corners, but maintain a steady effort and enthusiasm. You won't do this every day, but you must try to do it as much as you can. There will be times that you will be inactive for long periods and then you will come back with the optimism you started with. A letter in the mail box, a check, a request for product information, something will bring you back into the business and you'll learn more and more, and hopefully earn more and more too. But it will take many, many days. And, if I'm wrong, and you make a fortune overnight, that's great too. You can write a book and tell the rest of us how you did it and what your secrets were.

Make Everyday Count

This is good advice for business and for life. Make every day count as much as you can. Many days will be squandered and pass into the big circular file of time without anything to show for it we all know, but the majority of your days must produce something valuable to you. You must learn something every day or it is a lost day. Even when you watch TV, you can learn from the way advertising is presented.

When you read magazines from now on, you will study the mail order ads in the rear of the publication and examine them for content not just as a casual reader. Study the ads in your local newspaper and study your junk mail. Learn why junk mail is called junk mail, and why sometimes it is an art form. Why did you open the junk mail envelope? How was the envelope designed? Send away for information offers that appear in the classified sections. Study how they answer your request. Is there another way that you would do it better?

Learn from everything that happens to you in your day. You will waste a lot of time during the day as we all do following bad habits we learned as kids. We will goof off before starting to work. Distract ourselves by listening to the radio or reading an article or lingering on the Internet. Too often we lose precious time. Which can't be replaced.

MAILING LISTS

General

You will start creating your own mailing list as soon as you're getting orders for or inquiries about products you are advertising. The list will contain the names and address of all your customers and those prospects who just ask for information. This list will be the most important to you because you will have built it from personal experience. These are the people who trust you to return a good product for the money they sent you and they expect you to take care of them with new products you may sell.

The small mail order operation could take years to build a good list of several thousand names or sooner if the business really takes off. At the end of your first year you may have several hundred names of customers who have bought various products from you or asked about your product. This is your house list which you will build on every time a new customer is added. Without it you do not have a direct mailing target unless you rent a list from a list broker. List brokers are easy to reach and charge money for their rentals. Lists are not guaranteed to succeed and can cost you a pretty penny if you don't get the right target to aim at with your mailings. So be careful in this regard.

A good computer comes in very handy, almost indispensable, at this point of compiling mailing lists. Mailing lists change every day with additions, removals and changes of address. You must keep it up to date or it will become costly sending mail to wrong addresses. With a computer you will also have to the capability to print labels and mail envelopes with your sales information. You will soon see that if you have a thousand names that it will require a lot of input to keep the list current.

Rented lists are available in a variety of categories including recent mail order purchasers. You can rent a list of seniors, juniors, doctors, lawyers, truck drivers, nurses, and teachers and on and on. The professional broker will select a list closest to your requirements. Usually to minimum rental will include 5,000 names and could cost $75 to $100 per thousand names depending on the quality of the list. Mailing to a thousand names is not an easy job for the beginner, nor is it cheap. Just figure out the stamp requirements, (I don't know the price at the time you read this but at the time I write it is 37 cents for a stamp.) When I first wrote this book the stamp was under thirty cents. If you have ever sent out a thousand pieces of mail you know what a job it is. If your holiday list is a hundred names just times it by ten. This is assuming a one ounce content in the envelope. If you send more than three ounces of sales information or a small catalog the mailing cost rises. Check with the Post Office.

At the beginning you will be mailing only a few items, and that is the time to familiarize yourself with the basics of shipping and handling. You will become very selective when the expense of mailing hits home and you won't want to waste your time and money on every name that you have but try to select the ones that seems most promising, i.e., those that have given you the most business.

The arithmetic is easy, let's say your sales literature weighs enough to cost you a dollar and twenty five cents. That's $1250 for a thousand pieces of mail. If you mailed to everyone on a five thousand name list it costs you $6,250. If two percent return with orders they better be big ones to cover this type of expenditure. So don't do it unless you are sure of what you are doing and you won't be for a long while yet.

Does it make you wonder how some of these large companies can afford sending out the junk mail they do? Some packages I get cost the sender three bucks and change and I chuck it in the recycle bin without opening it. What a waste.

When you are beginning to mail several hundred pieces frequently you could explore the use of third class bulk mailing with the post office to qualify for a reduced rate. This will save you some money but you will have to sort your mail as the post office requires to save them time and save you money. The post office people will tell you about the feasibility of doing this.

They will issue you what they call an indicia (stamped number) that can be stamped or printed on an envelop in lieu of stamps. You also must band your mail in proper amounts and deliver it to the post office for mailing in special bags with arranged zip codes etc. Your local post office will be glad to give you the details including the necessary fees. This does not really begin to pay off until you are established and have large mailings. At that time you can check with the postal people to find out the details and the current rules, regulations and rates.

FINDING A LIST

Your local yellow pages will list mail list rental agents in your area. Also, check the Internet, YAHOO.com, and search for mailing lists of a wide variety. Finding a list rental broker is easy to do. Cooperate with your list broker to find the list suited for your sales pitch and products. He will want to give you good results so that you give him future business. Try to get the list that reflects interest in your products, its price range, and all other similarities you can match.

Many in mail order believe that the people of California and the other western states are receptive to mail order offers and make their mailings to those states first to test the product. My personal experience has been that this was true, but I also found that New England and Florida were also good selling States for my products. Unless it is a sun related product I don't see why Californians should buy anymore than New Englanders. Basically we are all built about the same. There are too many variables in testing regions that are not going to be your concern, or mine. We'll leave this area for the big shots.

RENTING A LIST

If you feel you must rent a list and the time is now, okay, but let me tell you a few things to do. First try to rent a list of a thousand names only to keep you costs low. This amount of names will not give you a true indication of the pull your product will have but it will be enough to get you acquainted with the mechanics of mailing. Try to get a list of previous mail order buyers if you can. Make sure the names are "clean", not old. Demand this from your broker. Remember you are renting the list for only one shot mailing and you must not copy the list to use a second time. If you get a buyer you may use the customers name again. It may be difficult to rent only a one thousand name list, but it is possible.

Lists may be rented with names printed on bond paper from which you will have to copy or cut out and paste onto an envelope for mailing, or they may be printed on pressure sensitive paper which can be peeled off and glued on an envelope. Also, some list houses will sell you lists on computer run off tapes. The list broker will explain his system to you and it costs you nothing to listen.

If you do rent a list, buy the pressure sensitive labels for your first mailing. Stuff a sample envelope and get it weighed at the post office before you continue with your mailing to check out the weight of the mailing. You may want to add some more literature to your envelope if the weight permits and is within the amount that you want to spend. The cost of mail increases as its weight increases but if you're within the weight allowed and can add a piece free of charge, do it.

Once again, your best list is the one that you have built for your own operation and I would suggest using this one before renting a strange list. As you add names to your list, you should list them under various categories such as buyers, inquires, state, product bought and how much was spent.

These are essential groupings. I also enter any other history about the customer that I think is important for future sales, such as color preferences, age, and other personal information that you may know.

The better you know your customers the better you will be able to serve them.

As you continue mailings, you will find that your customers are moving all around the place at an amazing frequency, and all this moving is playing havoc with the integrity of your list. If you do not update your list after every mailing, you will soon be the frustrated owner of lists that are full of non deliverable mail.

Nothing irks one so much as to make a large mailing with the hopes of sales to find your own envelopes coming back with the message stamped in red, "address unknown", "no forwarding address requested", or "would not accept mail". If you have enough of these returns you will see your money flying out the window and that's got to hurt.

Direct mailing, sending mail to your prospects in the hope of their becoming customers, is a personal type of marketing in my estimation. Professional direct mail marketing requires the input and talent of many people including graphic artists, printers sales experts, marketing professionals and many others. Large corporations have internal staffs to do this work, or they contract with other firms that specialize in direct marketing. And here you are trying to do it all by yourself as a beginner. You've got to have guts.

The least you should do is learn all about the operation that you can so that you master the basics. Think frugality, and think about waging small programs that don't overwhelm you. Just look at all the direct mails you get in your mail box every week. Notice the different colors, designs, and print that are used to get your attention? Even the experts don't know what is going to work for them. They try everything possible. With all the gimmicks and colors and shapes sometimes the plain, hand addressed envelope is the one mostly likely to be opened. But who is going to sit down and write out a hundred envelopes by hand? I did. It did not prove anything other than it is a lot of work. Just be conservative and take your time.

DROP SHIPPING

GENERAL

One of the reasons for my writing this book was to fill the need for a basic book that would address the small business entrepreneur and not assume there is a lot of cash ready to be invested. The books that promise the reader that they can make millions by starting a mail order business on a shoe string were really not written for those with limited resources who want to start in a very small way. The other reason for writing it was to explain the various aspects of drop shipping offered to beginners that can in some cases be valuable and in others cause them pain.

The newcomer eager to get into mail order often buys promises that are impossible to achieve. Having read the books and participated in drop shipping programs offered by various organizations, I know that they often exaggerate and disappoint. I ask you to be wary and examine closely before you get involved, and if you do, do it cautiously.

MAKE A MILLION BOOKS

Those books promising millions in mail order or indicate it is an easy business to start and operate do not address the problem of the average beginner who has limited resources and little business experience. Too often they include examples of business requirements that are beyond the means of the beginner. Exotic and expensive advertising scenarios are outlined in which the beginner will never participate, or if he does he would lose his shirt. Extensive testing and marketing programs are suggested, and that the beginner would not be able to afford. It appears to me that these books are written for those in a higher financial position or organizations with considerable funds; not for the person working alone trying to start a small business.

TYPES OF DROP SHIPPING

Some outfits sell the mail order novice training programs, catalogs and products to start a business all rolled up in one. These drop shipping outfits advertise in many magazines where the ambitious and eager person can read the ads on how to start a mail order business in several easy lessons. The lessons contain some very basic and often exaggerated instructions on starting a business. It works like this. After you have taken the lessons that were sold to you by the vender they will sell you catalogs that have your company name on the cover. You mail the catalog to your prospects and when a customer buys a catalog item you send the order to the drop shipper and he mails the product to your customer. You keep a percentage of the sale. This business offer is very tempting to accept, but should be examined carefully before you do.

Remember we spoke about a drop shipping arrangement with a vender at the trade show in New Hampshire. And how they listed our product in their catalog. That is okay. That can work fine. They place your product in their catalog and when they get an order from their customers, they will ask you to ship the product either to them or directly to the customer. The sale cost and profit is split as agreed between the two parties. In our case we had a birding product but no catalog and were glad of the opportunity to get the exposure in a large birding catalog. The catalog owner had many birding items to sell and felt that ours would be a good addition to his product line and took a chance on printing it in his catalog. It was beneficial to both parties who gained by this drop shipping scenario. This is a good business arrangement and nothing wrong there.

The drop shipper who offers you a catalog filled with his products, sells you catalogs in various quantities, (the more you buy the cheaper each catalog), offers an operation that should be closely examined.

They print your name on the catalogs that you buy and then you mail the catalog to your customers and prospects.

When you are starting from the bottom in mail order as I expect your are, there appears to be some advantages about this type of drop shipping offer, such as getting a variety of products quickly to sell in addition to the ones you find for yourself. Also, you don't have to buy and store a lot of products and you get a catalog which would be too expensive for a start up to afford and risk. But in the long run these advantages will not be sustained.

For these "advantages" you divide the profits from the sales and have no control of what product is listed in the catalog. The catalog cost and mailing can run up a big tab. The catalogs that are pre printed for many other start ups like you are all the same with the same product offered for sale. Only the name on the cover of the catalog varies according to the company that bought it. You just hope the same customer or prospect does not get the same catalog from two different companies or more. It would look strange to have three or four of the same catalog with different names imprinted on them. I would be embarrassed if one of them were mine.

However, to develop a similar catalog by yourself would be a very big cost and only attempted by someone or a group that has a lot of financial backing and a track record in the business. This is not the way for the beginner to go. Having a ready made, attractive catalog with your company name printed on it may be good for your ego, but really could end up with your losing your shirt.

The cost of joining a drop ship operation could cost you several hundred dollars depending what is offered and what you agree to buy. Some will sell you their "secrets" along with the drop ship agreement. They will sell you training instructions and study lessons. You can see from their perspective these companies have an interesting business situation going for them by selling you instructions, catalogs, stationary and products which you have to market.

If used cautiously these drop ship services can be of some small help to the beginner as an educational exercise, but for the most part they will be costly and of questionable value.

Remember, a drop ship catalog in these operations will cost you several hundred dollars to buy since they usually are offered in large quantities not just ten or twenty at a time, and the mail costs can add up. If you buy a catalog for a dollar, and mail it out for a dollar and a quarter, you can see that a hundred catalogs bought and mailed will cost you $225 a thousand catalogs just add three zeros to the number. $2,250, that's right. Very likely the catalogs sell for more than a dollar today.

Another weakness of this type of drop ship operation is that the products listed in the catalog will not always be available to sell. If this happens you will have to return the money and explain to the customer what the story is. This can be frustrating and a hassle when you don't know in advance that the product is out of stock. You then have to return the money to your customer explaining what went wrong. The drop shipper does not reimburse you for any expenses due to this situation.

Remember a forty page catalog may contain 200 or more items and if ten percent of them are out of stock you have to mark up your catalog or paste corrected pages to indicate this fact to the customer. This does not look good in the catalog and is not businesslike. Another short coming of this drop ship operation for you is that you have no control over the quality of the product. Not infrequently these products have been of shoddy quality in my experience and not worth the price they are sold for. There is nothing you can do to change this situation once you are committed to it.

You must ask yourself, would I buy this product for someone in my family? If the answer is no, what makes you think others will buy it from you, and even if they did, would you be proud in cheating the customer, and will he ever buy from you again?

If after all I've said here does not persuade you about not going into the drop ship operation where you buy catalogs and products from the same vender, at least remember to ask the vendor how long he expects his catalog to be current, and how many of the products will remain available. Also look at the numbers. The mark up of the product that goes to you minus the cost of the catalog, the mailing and other fees involved. Does it look like you will make a profit? I doubt it and so will you if you keep a clear head.

For the beginner who needs a catalog for his products I would suggest investigating the possibility of producing a simple, well prepared publication that you produce yourself as I spoke about earlier. Although not inexpensive, it would be better than the drop ship catalog. Better still, if you have several products that are related in use you may try preparing a flyer which will picture all the products on one side and give details of the description on the other.

I did this with a group of products for bird watchers when I was working with Tom Wong. These products included the Seat Bag, spotting scopes, walking cane and binoculars. All were photographed as a group and then printed on a glossy sheet of paper 8½ X 11 inches. The product description was printed on another sheet. It covered all the products we had to sell within a target group. All aspects of the flyer were professional and we did not need a catalog. This sales/sheet flyer was good enough to introduce our products and inexpensive to mail.

The basic essentials are in these pages and they will help you stay in the right direction. Go easy and be careful. Ask questions about anything you don't understand, use your head and you will not get hurt.

LAST, BUT NOT

BUSINESS PLANS

Usually a discussion of a business plan appears at the beginning of a business proposal, but I didn't want to go into details about preparing a business plan in this book because the information is available in other sources which I mention below. The development of a business plan is probably one of the most important things that you should know about for the new venture. There are books on this subject in your library and book store. A business plan outlines the direction your business is expected to take, the money that you have available to invest, the background of those involved in the venture, and puts all the components of the your project together for you and your backers to consider.

A good business plan will help you if you want to do business with a bank or other money lenders. Most banks will not loan money to you unless you have a business plan, so you can see how important this is for obtaining loans. In this book I assumed that the beginner I was talking to would have the money to finance his business out of his own pocket and did not want to be talking about bank loans and other murky subjects. But let's face it, there may be times when you just have to borrow money to expand or even start a business and if you will need money from another source you will need a business plan.

Your local Small Business Administration office is a good place to get further help on learning about and developing a business plan. Some States have an organization called SCORE, which stands for Service Corps of Retired Executives, which is made up of volunteers who work with the SBA and are certified small business volunteers. There are over thirteen thousand of these groups nationally and it would be a good idea to get in touch with one if you have a unit nearby. They will help you develop a business plan if you wish.

The basic Standard parts of a Business includes:

A concise description of the project you want to undertake.

Bio of the owner or owners.

Legal structure, and your lawyer and accountant.

A Marketing Plan.

Financial plan and your resources.

Supporting documents.

There are more areas you may cover, but this gives you a feel for it. You see why a bank likes business plans to work from before lending money. Even if you don't use a business plan to begin your business it would be a good idea to learn a little about them.

THE RIGHT STUFF

Perhaps I should have included this area at the beginning of the book too, but I did not want to scare anyone away from reading beyond these self-evaluations. To start a business, any business, you must have honesty and integrity. Everyone will admit they have these attributes, I'm sure.

After those qualification you must get along with people, have energy and be willing to work long hours. You must be disciplined, orderly, and punctual and have the ability to work alone.

Anybody who answered "yes" to any of these questions has the right stuff. If you did not, you don't have it. But to tell the truth, I know a lot of business men who don't have all of those attributes and still seem to hang in there.

In you heart of hearts, if you know yourself to be a procrastinator you will have to change or you will not make it here. In mail order you will have to work at the drop of a hat when orders come in and you will work late at night. What you do today should have been done yesterday.

Your Library, Free, Helpful, Always There

How anyone can consider going into business, any business, without checking out the value of the local library is beyond me. In almost every town in America there stands the FREE public library at the disposal of the citizens. The information in these libraries is endless and they have professional people to help you find out what you want.

I've spent many hundreds of hours in my county libraries searching information that would help me in many ways. For instance, there are reference books that list all the newspapers in America, their circulation, staff, departments, circulation and many other facts. You can find a reference book on the newspapers in your state that could be of valued to you. You find books that list manufacturers who could have a product you can sell.

Information on tax preparation, during that dismal time of the year, is there as are the daily newspapers which you can read and save a lot of money. Most libraries have copy machines, and they have computers you can use if yours should crash. Libraries have so much to offer and are one of the biggest bargains for your tax dollar.

Bergen County in New Jersey has a cooperative system that allows you borrow books from any library in the system. You can do this in person or over the Internet right from home. What a wonderful service this is not only for business but for everyday living too. I hope your library has this service too or will have it soon. Reference books of course must be used at the library.

I remember when I was working hard one day getting my business started and I felt all cooped up in my home office and wanted a change of scene. No problem, a short walk to my local library and there I was in a private area, ready to go. Few think of this value when considering the library. It is an office away from home and much more.

I mentioned that it would be a good idea to study as many magazines you can get your hands on. You won't be able to read them all because there are too many. But your library will have a collection that will keep you busy for a while studying the ads and the magazine itself. If you visit several libraries you will be able to study many periodicals that are valuable to the mail order person.

I've never met a library that I didn't like or a reference librarian who was not generous with her/his time. If we had to pay for these services directly we would appreciate them more.

Note: Barnes&Noble is also a good source for national magazines carrying many that your library may not have. You can look through them free, and buy one or two once in a while and give them some business.

800 Numbers

The use of toll fee telephone numbers for your customers is a very good idea because it opens up a twenty four hour a day coverage for your office. If you are working from home you will need a separate line for this service. The telephone companies offer various programs for this phone service and they change often. Basically the charge is a per-minute charge for the amount of 800 calls you get on your line with a monthly minimum charge. You will not need this service to begin and only consider it once you are a little more established.

The value of the 800 number to you can only be decided when you try it out and see what business it brings in versus the cost of the service. There is no argument that the 800 line offers you office coverage when you cannot be at the phone and may pick up sales that you could have miss. In my experience, the 800 number was great value. Many times people would leave a message with an order on the phone answering machine with their credit card number included.

It is always a good idea to return calls to verify them. Call back any person who leaves a message on your machine to check spelling of the name, address and other information in the order. It is also good public relations or customer relations to meet your customer voice to voice. I always try to convey a sense of honesty, enthusiasm and optimism when I speak to someone on the phone. I try to reassure them that they are buying the right product and that we are a good company to buy from. I don't push a sale obnoxiously, but rather try to reassure the customer that the product is right for him and that his money is returnable without questions in 30 days. You should do the same with your customers.

Using the phone is the closest that we get to our customers in this business. I would suggest using a technique on the phone that benefits you and your business. Have each call end with a smile and a trust of good business being done. I have no problem in asking the person who calls from Seattle how the weather is and whether it is raining again, or the lady from South Carolina, how many grandchildren she has. We get to be friends before the call is completed and that is good business.

Credit Cards

This is another valuable business service that you will have to decide on once you get established and determined its worth to your operation. Possibly you can do without it or postpone it until after you test your business activity for a while. If, however, you find that it would be of value in your sales, then check out the various offerings, terms, and read the small print closely. Know what you are getting into and the cost involved.

The costs you pay for this service will have to be added to the price of your product as are all the other costs you incur in doing business. Make sure that you are getting a fair price and a fair deal.

Repeating Myself

I will repeat here the caution necessary to start your business on a small scale. Frugally use whatever resources you already have at your command. Use your own home as your office base, use your computer if you have one and your car and any other equipment such as office furniture that may be adaptable. If you don't have something you need consider second hand shops, garage sales and clearance sales as opportunities to buy needed materials and equipment. You will find many opportunities to do this, take them.

Select a product line that you can realize a high mark up and that can be bought in small quantities to conserve your capital. Your product should have a wide appeal. It should be easy to wrap and ship. Buy it from a reliable supplier if you can find one. Remember you will be at his mercy when you reorder, if his price keeps jumping up every time you reorder it can play havoc with your customer relations.

Remember it is a good idea to find a secondary supplier for a product. The price that you pay for a product is not the only consideration. Consider the suppliers delivery and dependability history. If your supplier is very dependable and his deliveries are good you can live with him if his price is a little higher than the next guy, but not too much higher either. Use your common sense.

With a computer you don't have to be a genius to develop your own sales literature. Using copy from the supplier or manufacturer you can design your flyers and other sales literature very quickly with a professional look. When you print copies of your sales literature, use the quick copy shops and print in small quantities. You can always go back and print more. If you print more than is needed, you've wasted money.

Only advertise with classified ads or small display ads when you first start. Send for media kits from all magazines you intend to possibly advertise in and check out the prices for the space being offered. Remember media kits are one of the free opportunities that are being offered to you. Take it.

Sources of cheap and free information is provided to you from the US Printing Office with publications for small business operators, the libraries with source information of all kinds, the post office with rate and other information concerning third class mail, and advertising departments of most magazines who want to see you as a customer. You will learn more than you can imagine.

Using the local libraries is like money in the bank. You can use their space for study, going over your accounts and preparing information for your ads without charge to you. There is always a small quiet area in a library where you can do some research and reading. You get a good part of your real estate tax back when you take advantage of library facilities.

At your disposal in the library is the reference librarian who will help you with a project, reference books, publications, telephone directories, publicity sources, and much more.

Don't underestimate the power of a press release. With a little effort and cost you can get your product mentioned all over the country. I've written press releases for a variety of products including false alarm systems, odorless garlic tweezers seat bags and many more as I discussed earlier. The releases always included something of interest that an editor could possibly use. Nothing in the releases guaranteed they would be published, but I tried to make them short, and free of mistakes and easy for an editor to use. It is not magic. If you have a press release with a little interest in it you will succeed in placing it in a publication. If it is printed you will get free advertising, and perhaps sell some products. The editor gets a free story.

I could've added at least fifty pages to this book by copying information that is available to you in detail from the Government Printing Office, the Government Copyright Office, the Post Office, the Small Business Administration, the UPS, IRS, and a variety of other sources. I have not, to save you and myself some money. I've tried to give you the essentials without a lot padding. I've tried to make it simple and interesting.

HAVE A LOT OF FUN

You can have a lot of fun in mail order by using your ingenuity and watching your business planning and promotions develop into solid financial returns. You will be meeting new friends at conventions, shows and events associated with your business. I have enjoyed all this. You can also create a lecture on how to start a mail order business for your local adult school programs and community college. It is a way to meet more people, sharpen your ideas against the thoughts of others, have fun and make a few dollars. I've done this too and found the contact with aspiring business people very rewarding and enjoyable.

At the end, when it is all over, and some day it will be, I think it is more important to say I had a lot of fun rather than I made a bundle of money. But if you do both, that's just fine. Keep busy, work hard, have fun, and don't lose your shirt.

End

0-595-24387-8

Printed in the United States
141964LV00001B/125/A